BULLY, INC.

by Peter Burnett
with Jonathan Richards

BULLY, INC.

BULLY, INC.

Your Definitive Guide to Neutralising and Eliminating the Workplace Bully

Written by Peter Burnett with Jonathan Richards

ISBN 9780993227271

First published in 2019
Second edition published 2020

Bully, Inc. is an imprint of Leamington Books, Edinburgh, Scotland

Typeset in Garamond and Bebas Neue Bold
Author photograph by Ryan McGoverne

CONTENTS

ACKNOWLEDGEMENTS

Warmest thanks to Rachael Wallace Lane for showing me how value-based workplaces and individuals are the safest and most productive. She and her team, and others who have developed this approach, have created a fail-safe model that ensures well-being at work.

Thanks to Nikki Williams and the People Experience Team at Lush Limited. You were welcoming and demonstrated the most affirming determination to be the best when it comes to the happiness of your staff. Here's to 'putting people first.'

I would like to thank the Scottish Centre for Conflict Resolution and author Sarah Hussain for her advice and commentary. Warm thanks go to The Cyrenians, who allowed me to spend a day observing their work practices.

I would like to thank contributors Mary O'Neill of Amaranth Counselling & Psychotherapy; Gabriella Clarke of Mind Health Movement, who generously contributed their time and expertise; Chantal Gautier, Chartered Psychologist, and author of *The Psychology of Work: Insights Into Successful Working Practices* (Kogan Page); to Dr Sam Farley of the University of Leeds, who shared with me his work on cyberbullying, which was both guiding and informative; to business influencer Ted Coiné who provided generous, and valuable commentary; and to Janice White of The Empowered Employee, for comment and encouragement.

Thanks go to Ian White for generating The Bully Premium Calculator.

I would also like to thank Senior Advisor at ACAS Ron Inwood. I was privileged to see an early version of *Bullying Behaviours At Work: Understanding The Unacceptable*, and our subsequent conversations were most helpful.

Thanks go to my wife and best friend Arlene for support and love. Yours forever to share fun, music and comfort.

Special thanks to Jonathan Richards, without whom there would be no BULLY, INC. Also to the management at The Principal, Charlotte Square, Edinburgh.

Kindest thanks go to Susan White, Jill Hughes, Adele Telford, Lesley Storm, Jane Goldman and leadership coach Sam Pringle. Your advice was invaluable and has been fed into this project, and you have all been helpful in many different ways.

Thank you to Graham Goulden, John Housego and Dr Gary Namie who introduced ideas to me, helped me reach my conclusions, and brought to my attention new and enlightened considerations concerning this subject.

My thanks also to those of you whom allowed me to use your stories. I have always felt this book was a group effort. Thank you. I add that despite this, I take responsibility for errors, opinions (unless otherwise stated) and the accuracy of all data and quotations presented.

Peter Burnett, Edinburgh 2020

INTRODUCTION

MISSION

The mission of BULLY, INC. is to lay bare the mechanics of bullying behaviour in the workplace and beyond. We lift the lid on an epidemic problem and place everything on the table.

For the first time there will be clarity. The millions affected are not an inevitable collateral damage on the way to the consumer paradise. They amount to one person in four at a reasonable estimate, and for the first time, we will also show you what their suffering is costing our economy.

A large group of experts and others have contributed to this book and helped lift that lid. Heather Hodsen, author of *Women Who Hate Other Women* (2018), is one of them and she brought with her this provoking quote from employment rights expert Lewis Maltby:

> "Bullying is the sexual harassment of 20 years ago: everybody knows about it but nobody wants to admit it."

Looking back at the treatment of women that was ubiquitous only two to three decades ago, we can at least now explain why attitudes and behaviours persisted. Firstly, we didn't have the language to describe what was happening. In fact some of our language contained the assumptions that made ignoring sexism the norm as opposed to the exception. Then there was a lack of confidence about the subject. Not only did nobody speak up but there were no conditions laid out for the conversation, not in the media, nor in any obvious social sphere. It took decades for society to gravitate towards a coherent position where sexual harassment, now with its own identifying label, was exposed as something that would not be tolerated.

The tension surrounding the subject of bullying at work, this decade's 'sexual harrassment' as identified by Maltby, can be eased. We argue that talking about bullying is the only way to make a difference. And would it surprise you to know that the term 'sexual harassment' didn't even exist before 1975, when it was coined by journalist Lin Farley?

Prior to that, how could we tackle something — that we couldn't even name? As a result and because so few would talk about sexual harassment — millions suffered. That is why we talk about bullying behaviour at BULLY, INC. and describe it fully, cleanly, and with no grey areas. We know that uncensored and open discussion enables things to change.

What do we think about when we hear the word 'bully'? Maybe we don't know what to say, because we have so few tools to deal with this overpowering word. Yet in avoiding talking about bullying, we enable it.

We all deserve much better. We want change. And maybe BULLY, INC. can be a start.

BULLY, INC.

BULLY, INC. is a fading, dysfunctional work setting that too many of us know too well. At BULLY, INC. this 'bullying' thing belittles us in person and by text, and once in a while it drives an employee out of the door, never to return.

It excludes and it shouts and it wounds targets, making the rest of us complicit in their suffering.

Advancing technology means bullying can cut at workers 24/7 in a ceaseless cycle via social media, texts and apps, so for some there are zero hours respite.

It plagues the workplace. Even the institutions charged with passing laws that define workplace bullying are embroiled in accusations and testimonies. The UK Parliament is not immune, even going as far as to suppress internal investigations via its own Parliamentary privilege.

Infected workplaces are everywhere. You may well work in one. Statistically, you probably do.

The British National Health Service (NHS) has been long acknowledged as a bully's paradise. Gigantic infrastructure with clear hierarchy. Right now, a mid-wife with a 30-year career is being dragged over the coals for her choice of hair colour. (In her case, red).

Great British Bake Off? Cosy as a cream tea on a Winter's afternoon? Not according to the boss of the production company responsible for the show, which has now migrated to Channel Four, who described previous BBC executive bosses as 'the biggest bullies'.

And the former owner of one of the biggest high street stores faces multiple claims of bullying, from employees and journalists.

What has happened? Has it always been like this? Or is snowflake culture making us softer? Less tolerant? Less grin-and-bear-it? Less accepting?

This book, BULLY, INC. dissects what bullying means specifically for the workplace in the 21st century. What it looks like. What it feels like.

It highlights the health impact of bullying and mistreatment in the workplace, and how cardiovascular problems are directly linkable to bullying as well as a multitude of mental health issues that follow when the workplace is an environment of manipulation and fear.

Our book identifies inspired new models and practices that strike at the very core conditions of bullying, literally leaving bullies with nowhere to go.

And it shows how even the world of celebrity has its own bullying issue, and how 'bullytainment' is a real, living thing.

This book, BULLY, INC. looks out on a rapidly evolving workplace where change is inevitable and will reshape what working in the 21st century will feel like for millions.

Moreover, it discovers the generation that may just be the silver bullet for bullying in the workspace — a demographic not accepting of finger-pointing, raised voices, emotional abuse, manipulation or being marginalised in any way. This is a place not unlike ethical cosmetic business giant Lush — a business that has held on to company values established in the mid-90s at its foundation. A company actively looking out for its employees and totally persuaded of the desirability of the organic benefits that accrue from a contented and listened-to workforce — where making a mistake is not a trigger for withering comments and derision.

Imagine that freedom. Imagine how that must feel. And now believe these types of values are heading our way.

BULLY, INC. anticipates a struggle, but sees it underpinned by commercial realism and the shifting sands of the tolerance levels of our emerging generations who are not willing to accept falling emotional debris as the price of doing (dysfunctional) business.

BULLY, INC. will soon be no more.

MEETING THE WORKPLACE BULLY

By the time we're adults we've already seen bullying at home and at school, so when we pretend it doesn't happen at work, we betray ourselves as well as those that have been singled out. In a way, we're all experts when it comes to bullying behaviours. We are either let down by institutions which favour bullying or we're too scared to become involved. We all know what bullying looks and feels like, because it resides in our oldest memories. We are experts.

Workplace bullying is slowing society down. It costs the UK economy up to £20 billion a year, according to arbitration service ACAS. This figure only considers lost productivity, absences and staff turnover and it doesn't include the subsequent epidemic of mental health problems. ACAS itself receives 20,000 calls a year related to workplace bullying in the UK alone.

The good news is that we have a newly empowered generation to show us how to make our workplaces safer, and independent help is also at hand, in the shape of a robust and failproof system of shared values.

The bad news is that bullying can be normalised so

quickly that sometimes we can't even see it when it's taking place. This is an issue for everyone and so the more books about workplace bullying that appear, the more blog posts that are published discussing bullying and the more people that speak about bullying and mistreatment in general — the more likely we are to get on top of it.

The last people to see any of this are of course are the bullies themselves. To them other people are the problem — which is why a straightforward guide to bullying behaviours is needed.

We must all learn to be honest about what is and what is not bullying behaviour and be prepared to go about things differently when we uncover it.

Any team or business can be degraded to the point of closure by bullying. A tech start-up I observed at close quarters was halted in its tracks because of the bullying behaviour of one of its owners. As is often the case, the most competent and ethical employees were the first to go and after that had happened, a decline set in that ensured the business would collapse — which it did.

At the opposite end of the spectrum, I have interviewed several 21st century companies which have prioritised staff well-being and have flourished as a result, and in one case gone global.

The difference is stark and yet the lessons are easily summarised — bullying persists because there is an unwillingness to discuss it, often because we don't know exactly what it is we are dealing with.

Managers need to know what constitutes bullying behaviour, as do staff. For some managers and business owners, the issue of bullying is non-existent, because these owners and managers feel that what they say goes. Commonly, these bullying business owners and managers are rewarded for bullying behaviour and not sanctioned for their conduct. This can apply to small businesses everywhere, to teams and departments within corporations, as readily as it can be exposed and discussed in the highest political offices in the world.

Bullying behaviours persist in so many places because bullying often achieves results, and although statistics vary from place to place and between different industries, around a half of incidents of workplace bullying conclude with a targeted individual leaving their job against their wishes. This situation not only perpetuates the bullying, but it often sets the seal on bullying behaviours. That is why a person who has a reputation for bullying behaviour will usually be associated with multiple incidents of emotionally abusive conduct. That office shouter who has the temper tantrum doesn't just do it once — the reputation arises from repeat performances.

The fallout from these bad practices amount to health, social and financial costs that are nearly beyond measure, and which make tackling workplace bullying one of the most significant challenges of our time.

I believe that everyone has a workplace bullying story. I have worked for small companies, global firms, banks, several public utilities, an academic institution, a local council, a charity, for publishers, newspapers, shops, farms, courier services, pubs, restaurants, hotels and even in virtual reality and in the theatre — but the fundamentals I have witnessed regarding workplace bullying remain the same, whenever and wherever they surface.

The most common reason bullying takes hold in any workplace is because the conversation about bullying has not happened there. This may be for lack of clarity on the subject, or it may be because certain people don't want to talk about it. However, talk about it we must and so it's important to lay down some fundamentals. Some people will not even know that they are being bullied, and for others, questions might revolve around what is and what is not bullying.

To begin with, bullying behaviour always boils down to two constants:

1. Verbal, physical, emotional or psychological abuse is used in order to —
2. Achieve power over others and / or remove a targeted person's power or remove that person entirely.

This is a base-line description which can help anyone identify bullying behaviour. It is helpful that we all know what bullying is so we can look at ourselves as well as at others. Bullying at work varies with each workplace, but across all environments bullying is the same — it's a set of behaviours and bad practices. These behaviours and bad practices can be observed however, and because they can be observed, they can be dealt with and discussed. Unfortunately, as many have discovered, policies are not enough to prevent these behaviours and policies cannot save targets from workplace abuse, or any of us from bad habits and actions. Only the conversation can do that.

Bad practices in the workplace will include poor

communication, abuses of power and authority, and letting bullying take root and normalise. Counter-behaviours that will combat this will therefore include good communication, a focus on leadership (as opposed to power), and the introduction and maintenance of positive values.

Policies by themselves do not prevent harmful behaviours, and although they contain desired behavioural norms, failing to have regular conversations about the contents of those policies means that when someone gets away with some poor behaviour once, they will almost certainly begin to get away with it repeatedly.

This explains how what starts as bad practice can become bullying. This book does not set out to lambast bullies or point the finger, but will show how through a lack of values and understanding, bullying develops.

Bullying is different from aggression. Whereas aggression may involve a single act, bullying involves an on-going or repeated pattern of behaviour. Demanding bosses are not to be called 'bullies' so long as they remain both fair and respectful. So long as they are motivated by getting the best performance from those they work with, the same applies to managers and other colleagues who may appear abrasive.

Bullying is instead about things like impulse control, obsessions and targeting. It is usually about one person having an issue with another person, and their subsequent harmful actions. It is about that one person who won't be disagreed with and it is about fear. It is about poor management and blame, and it is about behaviour that someone resorts to because they do not share group values.

The best way for one adult to achieve power over

another adult is by belittling them, and this can be done almost unconsciously. A bullying individual does not always know they are a bully — and that's why they are best identified by their behaviours. While we may aim to neutralise these behaviours, we cannot deal with the factors that have made that bullying person what they are. What we can do instead, is have everyone agree upon some shared values, and we can refer to those values when we are in doubt about something someone has done.

This is because we are all capable of being blind concerning our own behaviour.

Certainly, there is no person who leaves for their job in the morning, thinking something along the lines of:

> *"I'm off to work to bully him again today."*

… although, some might think something such as:

> *"I'm going to take him down a peg or two today."*

Or:

> *"They're not getting away with their inefficiency any longer."*

Or:

> *"She's just not fit for this job and I'm going to have to pick up the slack."*

For better or worse, these are examples of what a bullying individual or a potential bully may be thinking.

Too often, the character of the bully is a distant figure — a symbol of evil and a person unknown. While a workplace bully is something nobody wants to think about, ignoring his or her logic will allow bad working practices to become the norm. The person who bullies is also a thinking and feeling individual as well as the rest of us, and for whatever reasons, that person has opted to use tools such as emotional abuse, because they cannot achieve their goals through other means.

It's for this reason that one of the most common criticisms of people who bully is that they are inefficient. This is also why it is common for bullies to target people who are efficient. Or as one target of a long-term campaign of bullying put it to me: "The bullies always go for the reasonable people."

Bullying is a way of getting things done, but by harmful means. The only part of that sentence that the bully sees is the part that says that things have been done. Fittingly, people who bully tend to have justifications when it comes to the harmful means, and this might often include blaming the target for their actions.

I would like workers to be able to identify bullying behaviour by looking for some easy clues which bullies can ill conceal. I'd also like bullying individuals to know that in costing our workplaces what they do, it is their behaviour that is at fault. Ideally, we may wish people who have bullied others to confront their behaviour, although this is not always possible. What we can do however is create the conditions where bullying is not an option.

That is why a value-based system guiding both behaviour and aims will squeeze the bad habits which lead to bullying out of any workplace. It will be a shock for some, but I am afraid to say that anti-bullying policies are not going to be enough.

Such a system of values however will establish some ground-rules for everybody, which will mean that such behaviour is not possible — far less permissible.

KEY FEATURES OF WORKPLACE BULLYING

Bullying involves observable behaviours and actions. This means it's easy to start the conversation about it. To start that conversation, here are some key features of bullying behaviour which show how we might like to think about it. The following four ideas present straightforward ways of understanding what is and what is not bullying at work, and they always apply to instances of bullying. These ideas are:

- It's Not the Issue That's at Issue
- Behaviour — Not Psychology
- Bullying is a Health Issue
- Bullying is an Issue for Everyone

The reality is that bullying is both simple and complex. Simple — insofar as its basics remain the same, whether it concerns the behaviour of a world leader or a manager across the corridor. Complex in that its expression depends on the people and the situation.

It's Not the Issue That's at Issue

Workplace bullying usually begins subtly and is based on a bullying individual's intent to break or remove another colleague or employee.

Technically described, bullying normatively consists of repeated, detrimental, damaging, health-harming mistreatment of another person by means of various types of abuse.

These will be emotional, verbal or physical abuses and will involve threatening, intimidating, humiliating or sabotaging behaviour.

This behaviour can go under the radar, or it can be in-your-face behaviour, as in the case of the 'office-screamer'.

Either way, bullies believe that a targeted individual is in and of themselves a problem.

This is why bullying individuals try hard to convince other people in the group that their target is a problematic person.

What bullies convince themselves is just as relevant. For a bully it is their business partner, or a certain employee, or whoever else it may be that is the problem.

Therefore, always bear in mind that it is *not the issue that is the issue with a bully* — but it is the other person.

This is how bullies transform dialogue around work-related matters into destructive behaviour which targets the person that is for whatever reason 'in their way'.

As an example, here is a case in which normal daily issues could not be resolved and so a working relationship escalated into mistreatment:

> "I was in a meeting and we'd been disagreeing on a few things — first it was how much to spend on social media then on whether or not to sack a certain employee. My business partner wasn't getting their way and abruptly stopped discussing the issue. I was then told I was unprofessional and that I knew nothing about social media. These statements were repeated in an email afterwards and circulated so that we ended up not talking about the job but my personality. My business partner stopped working with me on the issue and simply told everyone I knew nothing about my job. That was their way of ending the discussion. It was really undermining. And it was only the start." (Richard, 49, E-commerce Start-up)

While we can't call an isolated incident a campaign of bullying, when it continues — when the emails persist — when the backbiting persists — when the insults persist — then this is bullying behaviour.

Once that process begins there will be a noticeable impact on the physical and mental health of the target as well as an impact on the quality of their work. We have barely started to witness the bullying here and yet the cost is mounting, both in health and in damage to the business. This story also contains a key signifier concerning bullying behaviour — one person has been made the issue.

Whatever the job and whatever the project or workplace, it doesn't matter. The issue for a bully is the person that for whatever reason they do not like — the one they tell people "they cannot work with".

Quite simply: 'the other'.

Behaviour — Not Psychology

In every instance of workplace bullying a triad of parties is involved — the target, the bully and the bystander. All these work at BULLY, INC.

When a bully intimidates someone, they intimidate everyone. It's not just a powerful thought — it's a hallmark. If one person is bullying another in an office or workgroup, then that single bully may have managed to alter the entire workplace.

We've all met bullies. There's the archetypal figure of 'the school bully' — the individual that everyone is afraid of. We all know that individual from memory. The bullying parent is another archetype.

That person who has meltdowns in the office (shouting, desk thumping, berating etc.) are the same kind of archetype because everyone knows their reputation and is aware of what they are capable of. Although we may be scared of that person, we still as bystanders need infallible mechanisms which will check their behaviour. This is always about behaviour and never about psychology.

Yes, there are fascinating psychological qualities which accompany bullying behaviour, of that there is no doubt. People who bully tend to have poor impulse control, failings in competence, a skewed perception of rightness and messy home lives. But we must look in a neutral fashion not at bullying individuals as a type — but at their behaviour. Behaviour is observable and can be changed, whereas people's motives may be hidden. As for people's personalities, particularly the personality of bullies, we are in the workplace here, remember. Analysing bullying individuals' temperaments and psyches is a feat beyond most of our capabilities and one that could take months and even years, and still return an inconclusive result.

It is easy to find pithy quotes which state things like: "*Bullies are cowards at heart and may be credited with a pretty safe instinct in scenting their prey.*" (Anna Julia Cooper).

Not only does this handy quotation fail to tell us anything about bullying behaviour, how to cope with it and what its effects are, it also makes blanket psychological statements about bullying individuals, which those individuals will fail to appreciate and which may not even be true. In the workplace nobody should be bothered with the personality or circumstances of a bullying individual. Instead we can help that individual and those around them by focusing on behaviour and leaving it at that.

Finally, psychology may simply not work for bullies! Counsellor and psychotherapist, Mary O' Neill, whose Master's degree examined workplace bullying, points out simply that "bullies don't go to counselling." Nothing may change a bully's personality then. But as we will see, their behaviour is an entirely different prospect.

Bullying is a Health Issue

Most organisations today, large and small, have a thing called a Human Resources department. Not everybody knows what goes on in these HR Departments, but they are important nonetheless. The job of HR obviously varies from place to place, but in the most general terms, Human Resources has responsibility for issues related to the people within your organisation. HR might develop wellness initiatives, and provide guidance regarding disciplinary actions, and usually they also handle training programs, compensation and benefits.

If we have discovered one thing in the numerous instances of workplace bullying and mistreatment we have come across, it is that virtually all of these cases find their way to Human Resources departments which are ill-suited to dealing with them. This is not because these departments are not effective. Human Resources sections make numerous types of contributions and savings to their organisations. The issue is that dealing with instances of workplace bullying is not on the Human Resources checklist — and nor will it ever be.

This is because bullying is a health issue and not an issue of conflict. When one person yells at another, lies to them, sends abusive emails or carries out any of many bullying behaviours — this is not a conflict and so it cannot be mediated. Of course, bullying behaviour can be prepared for, for example in the form of training and information provided by Human Resources. But by the time any bullying behaviour is taking place, or felt to be taking place, management is required and not Human Resources. This often puts HR in a bad position too. Ask yourself if you have ever heard someone complain: "I took this bullying issue to HR and they were useless."

Well, that's not a fair use of Human Resources. Bullying is a management issue and as many thousands of individuals have found out to their detriment, Human Resources is not the place where bullying can be identified, remedied and stopped.

Bullying behaviour is, and always has been, a health and

safety issue. Allowing bullying to become an issue of mediation, or personality, or sending it to HR, has only ever allowed bullying to embed in a work culture.

Before it is anything else, bullying is a health issue.

That's why, once bullying has begun, it is sometimes hard to remedy. This is because usually, if a target of bullying discovers that they have been the subject of prolonged mistreatment, there is already a mountain on top of them that is going to be hard to move — especially if the bully is already out on top of the mountain with their flag dug into its peak.

Once bullying has established itself, it also normalises quickly, and becomes a culture. And this can happen on a micro scale just as it can happen on a corporate or even a national scale.

Digging a bully out of a company or workgroup can be costly, especially if the bully is the boss or owner. Bystanders may be unwilling to act and the corporate climate may already be established.

This is why some HR departments introduce company values to which everyone can ascribe. As a bystander to bullying it can be difficult to know what to do — who or what is 'right' — and how to protect yourself if you are going to stand up for someone who has been targeted.

This is when a set of values can do the heavy lifting. Such shared values can be the arbiters of behaviour and will be robust enough to take a pummelling. If one worker or manager is looking for a fight, then the company values can handle it. Employees shouldn't have to.

Values don't bruise. People do.

Bullying is an Issue for Everyone

Well-functioning values are not just for those who feel the need for protection from bullying. They are for everybody who wants to ensure that bullying will never happen where they work. Bullying is a problem impacting the work lives of millions. Even the World Health Organization acknowledges its prevalence: "Bullying and psychological harassment are well-known causes of work-related stress and related mental health problems." (Devora Kestel, Director, Mental Health, WHO).

On an individual level bullying behaviour creates sustained workplace misery; unfulfilled and stagnating careers; poor health, and indeed poor wealth. In the UK alone, the TUC (Trades Union Congress) has found that nearly one-third of the UK (29%) have admitted to being bullied at work (Survey, YouGov for the TUC to coincide with Anti-Bullying Week, November 2015).

While nobody is denying the scope of the problem, there are differences in opinion concerning how workplace bullying arises. Bullying is presented by some experts as an inherent aspect of bureaucracy and even a fundamental of capitalism, while for others it is a process grounded in the personalities of the individuals involved.

This is from writer and campaigner Sarah Hussain, the author of *The Secret Life of Bullies* (2016):

> "Bureaucracy and the cycle of bullying grind any opposition into more grist for the mill and — as with any repressive regime — eventually persistent disappointment becomes tacit acceptance and then

> active co-operation on the part of perpetrators, victims and witnesses, keeping all of them invested on the self-perpetuating fallacy that the person in charge must know what they are doing, simply by reason of being in charge in the first place."

This argument reflects the enormous and sometimes arbitrary power that corporate systems hand to certain individuals, usually because these individuals are perceived as tough and aggressive. In such cases, the author argues, large institutions with seemingly healthy Human Resources (HR) departments are emulating political dictatorships, which have historically displayed a 'primed, ready-to-use framework' which at root seeks to control people, rather than allow individuals to flourish.

In contrast, a 2012 survey from the Workplace Bullying Institute titled 'Why Workplace Bullying Happens', found a similar answer, but placed the emphasis on individual employers, some of whom it argued were willing to deal with the issue, while others because of their particular management culture, let bullying go unchecked.

The survey also found that most workers feel that laws to stop bullying are either absent, or too weak to be useful. The survey's author is social psychologist Dr. Gary Namie who, who is regarded as one of North America's foremost authorities on workplace bullying and he has this to say:

> "The absence of negative consequences (punishment) for bullies and lacking the will to stop it both reflect employer mishandling of bullying. Employers establish and maintain the work environment."

In summary, Dr. Namie found that from a self-selected sample of nearly 700 individuals with experience of being bullied at work, 56% attributed their bullying to the culture of the company at which they had received mistreatment, while 24% felt that bullying was inherent in certain people — and 20% felt that the issue was societal.

The points of agreement here are more significant than the differences, and while the question regarding 'why people bully' is of interest to psychologists, the truth is that bullying behaviour does not vary, wherever it is found.

We accept far too often that we live in a 'dog-eat-dog' culture and support competitive systems in which there are winners and losers. We meet people who have had bullying parents and we speculate on why it may be that they as adults resort to bullying behaviours too.

Although these are interesting discussions and we can agree or disagree, what we can be unanimous on however is what constitutes bullying behaviour. It is also a given that this behaviour when it takes place will affect us all — whether bully, target or bystander.

Proving that someone has used bullying behaviours to achieve their ends can be hard, especially when many workplace bullies cover themselves, sometimes arguing for example that their actions are for the benefit of the company or team. In unravelling this kind of situation, the dynamic between target, bully and bystanders is crucial. That is why bullying is an issue for everyone, no matter what their beliefs, and it's why the bystanders hold the key to resolution.

While laws against harassment and other abuses are necessary, it is still down to company owners and managers to put value systems in place which can stop bullying from ever taking hold — rather than have them relying on laws to either discourage it, or punish those who have been shown to have bullied others.

Values are free, and once agreed upon cannot fail to act as a common arbiter that apply to everyone, no matter where they may work in a company.

With that said, we'll look at the dynamics of our trio of employees — the target, the bully and the bystanders — and explain how a system of declared, shared and lived values will spare us the emotional, fiscal and psychological fallout from this global issue.

TARGET

Also known as: the subject, the injured party, the person who is bullied, the sufferer, the casualty, the scapegoat, the prey ... and in the most extreme of cases: the victim.

MEETING ROOM

I found my first real job when I was aged 14. This real job was in the television department of a local store and the reason that I knew that it was a real job was because we had meetings.

The popular American executive coach Joel Garfinkle, says that "the average employee spends about one-third of their work week in meetings, so they're the best opportunity you have to make your expertise known" — and he is correct.

Meetings are a sign that we are taking each other seriously and are often the most important parts of our day.

At meetings we find out what the company is doing and what's expected of us.

At meetings we get to know each other, and we have a chance to see each other in action.

When I had my first job I said nothing in the meetings, but there was always an opportunity when the chairperson or team leader would say at the end: "Are there any questions?"

This is one of the more important aspects of meetings at work — information about the company and our role will be passed on, but we should also have the chance to be heard. If we do not have the chance to be heard, then I do not believe it is a meeting.

Similarly, if anyone breaks the basic codes of the meeting scenario — for example by shouting in anger, storming out, or any other number of alarming and unusual activities — we may have a fair idea that this person is not quite at ease with the team model.

As I grew, I continued in different service roles, finding work in shops, bars and restaurants. I took up causal, full time and part time gigs like gardening, and other odd jobs including being a dishwasher, a hotel porter and that young person who hands out leaflets in the street.

Yet — in every case and in every job, no matter how unimportant I was in the overall structure, there were still meetings. Often these meetings were not treated seriously by some of the staff — especially those staff who may have been working in more menial positions. Still the meetings were a change of pace, a chance to see the boss in action, and figure out (or be told) one's place in the company scheme.

Later, when I began to take up office-based work, meetings took on a more formal and fuller tone. Meetings in office environments are usually pivotal and larger companies and public bodies acknowledge this by having specific meeting rooms. I began to understand that there were many different types of meeting — from planning meetings to team-building meetings, to what I would call status update meetings.

There are plenty of professions in which your work will consist entirely of meetings.

We all know too, that there are such things as good

meetings, even great meetings, and that from time to time there were also bad meetings. Bad meetings are 'bad' because even though people come together and try to progress matters, sometimes no way forward is achieved.

When I graduated to management and to hosting and chairing meetings in my 30s, I had experience enough to be aware of different types of people — including those observers and thinkers that don't speak up in meetings, as well as those that are always speaking.

This is a reminder that not everybody is the same — in fact we are incredibly diverse and different as a workforce. Those who are the conscientious and quiet type still have to work with people who may be talkative and outspoken, but nobody should be saying that anybody's qualities are better than anybody else's. This opinion is fertile ground for bullying behaviour and a risk to potential targets, who may start to feel that they do not fit in to a certain place, if they can't be heard. It's a reminder of the kind of equality that needs to persist in meetings, a reminder that everyone should be listened to, and in a proper manner.

Taking responsibility for meetings is quite a milestone in life. If you are hosting a meeting you are simply not just turning up — you are turning up and having to ensure that everyone has a good meeting. Having a good meeting is fortunately quite easy, so long as a few protocols are observed, and these include:

- We prepare
- We listen to each other
- We don't talk over each other
- And we don't raise our voices

When I began to own businesses rather than just working for them, the meeting became even more important. Whether we know it or not, we are always learning on the job and everything that I have so far learned I have done so through observation, through listening to others, and at worst through painful experience.

Bullying is one such painful experience, and although (and with good reason) literature on workplace bullying behaviour emphasises the needs of the target as the first consideration, there is more at stake. Notably, the wellbeing of the entire company or workgroup is at stake when any one person is bullied.

That is why BULLY, INC. begins in the meeting room, because this is where we can observe general dynamics and where the fundamentals of our personalities — for ill or good — shine.

Some meeting room scenarios operate on a survival-of-the-loudest basis where some people are simply not heard, and although this is not bullying, it is a dynamic to challenge. Similarly, in meetings, bullying behaviours that are already ongoing can be cemented, and done so in front of others, thus legitimising them.

The others here are the bystanders — generally speaking all of us at one time, and most of us most of the time. Bystanders have a part to play and a role in neutralising harmful behaviours because in combatting bullying behaviour, a target may be the last person that can help.

The target is the one being kept awake at night and sitting like an automaton on the train with the same unanswered questions scrolling before their mind's eye like an endless webpage.

If bystanders can help with answers here the difference will be momentous.

Holding a successful meeting is not hard and with this as a goal, and with values on hand, everyone's interests can be met. You might not think it need not be said, but it does: well-being is key.

It's put very well by business influencer Ted Coiné, co-author of *A World Gone Social: How Companies Must Adapt to Survive* (2014):

> "A happier workforce is a harder working, more creative, more loyal, and longer-tenured workforce. Dozens of books have catalogued this indisputable fact, and now there are numerous investment funds prospering from that truth as well."

Holding good, inclusive meetings at which we follow those four above rules is going to start us off, then. The fact that global investors are now aware of the fact that a bully-free workplace is a more profitable one — this should at the least indicate the road we must take.

E-TARGET / E-BULLY

What does bullying look and feel like? Visualise a spiky ball that can never be handled without it hurting. Even when the bullying is over and time has passed, the spikes still cause twinges and will pain the target whenever they think about the experience.

This is the image that abides for targets — something that always hurts, no matter how you handle it.

Therapists and academics have found that in the last decade, social media and other online activity have made this spiky ball of bullying not just larger than it has ever been — but potentially a 24-hour presence.

That's why there are no upsides to being a bully's target. Even on the rare occasions when bullies are identified, disciplined and their targets receive justice in the form of an apology or even compensation — even then, targets do not feel good. The damage is done.

Ditch The Label (ditchthelabel.org) addresses the frequency and nature of cyberbullying in the UK, uncovering an uncomfortable range of experiences in the process. This is done via an annual report, titled *The Annual Bullying Survey*, produced in conjunction with UK-based schools and colleges. The report gathers together 'the opinions and experiences of young people who are currently studying in high schools and colleges nationwide.'

In terms of cyberbullying among younger people, the survey found that the following percentages of people had experienced the following bullying behaviours:

- Had a nasty comment posted on their profile — 39%
- Had a nasty comment posted on their photo — 34%
- Were sent a nasty private message — 68%
- Had their profile wrongfully reported — 18%
- Had been bullied in an online game — 23%
- Had their private information shared — 24%
- Had somebody impersonate them online — 18%
- Had rumours about them posted online — 41%
- Had photos or videos of them posted that they didn't like — 27%

Cyberbullying is a new tech-driven phenomenon. It can happen between individuals as readily as other bullying, but cyberbullying has a serious potential for scale, and seemingly invisible or anonymous mobs can form, and quickly target individuals.

The closest historical equivalent to this might be found in the intolerant, informal associations of people within our historical communities, who through gossip, innuendo and other means targeted 'witches', or other non-conformists and outsiders. The ease and immediacy with which harm can now be done on social media is a massive step for organised bullying, however, and the damage, because it is generally unseen, is greater than most people imagine.

The larger micro-blogging and social network websites have in particular had a corrosive effect on our discourse and relationships, by appearing to exaggerate our impulses. And as bullying is both bad practice and a short cut at times, and often the result of poor impulse control, the temptation for bullies to send that angry email, or that gossipy text, is great.

This means that virtually no workplace bullying today occurs without a 'cyber' component — and this will intensify so long as technology develops and our reliance on it remains.

Much of the millennial generation prefer to work entirely by technology — as per those canvassed for a newspaper article on the subject (The Guardian '*Millennials at work: five stereotypes - and why they are (mostly) wrong*' (15.03.2016) who are 'able to do most of their work at home equipped with only a phone and laptop.'

Thanks to the COVID-19 pandemic of 2020, a large and as of yet undefined percentage of the workplace have joined them. This was an unexpected turn of events which means we must all ask with some urgency the following question: if the tools your bully favours are sitting right next to you and switched on all the time, then what are the consequences?

Occupational Psychologist and researcher into cyberbullying, Sam Farley, describes how bullying at work intersects with the use of technology:

> "Cyberbullying can be thought of as a specific form of workplace bullying, which is channelled exclusively through technology (e.g. email, telephone, social media). Much of what we know about traditional forms of bullying is also likely to be true of

cyberbullying. However, there are some important factors that differentiate cyberbullying, for example it can occur at any time, it can be seen by a much greater audience, and the perpetrator, target and bystanders are likely to be in different locations when it occurs. In the working context, there is also evidence that cyberbullying occurs less often than traditional bullying, which may be due to the fact that cyber behaviours leave a 'digital footprint' which targets could use as evidence that bullying has taken place. In the future it will be important to understand whether initiatives and interventions aimed at reducing traditional bullying, also work to reduce cyberbullying."

Sam Farley is right to identify behaviour as the issue, and points out that bullying continues to be bullying, regardless of the tools. He identifies technology as amplifying both the actions of bullying and the hurt it causes, and crucially he reports that targets are more vulnerable than they have ever been.

The question then appears to be which approach is likely to be the safest, and with the most positive results for all? That is — should we place the psychology of the bully or their behaviour as the centre of our focus? Farley says:

"We know from a large number of studies that the main cause of workplace bullying is the work environment. When a work environment is characterised by high job demands, low autonomy, laissez-faire leadership, role conflict and job insecurity,

> workplace bullying occurs more often. It is therefore primarily stressful working conditions that lead people to engage in bullying behaviour. This suggests that people who would not dream of enacting bullying behaviour are often driven to it by their working conditions and having an understanding of this may make a situation feel less personal for the target. Of course, there are some people who are predisposed towards engaging in bullying due to personality characteristics, however these cases are in the minority."

These 'personality characteristics' often play a part in what is called 'blame culture', which is when bullying individuals ascribe negative qualities to their targets and attack them on that basis. In practice, this includes a huge range of possible online activities, including email messages, tweets, the use of hashtags, and other types of posts which have the effect of eroding a target's self-confidence as well as being undermining in other ways.

Whatever the method, the targeting that is taking place in cyberbullying is amplified by the technology used. Bullying behaviour appears for most people who carry it out to have commonalities with obsession, or extreme interest. A bully will be at some level obsessing about their target — and social media and other internet services will provide material to fuel this.

This is why technology, social media and blame interlock so firmly when bullying behaviour is involved. First, there is the large amount of information available concerning each of us — some of it stored on company record and much of it is publicly visible. Then there is the fact that we have no idea who is looking at this material — and when.

As blame is important to workplace bullies, it's easy to see why technology exacerbates their abusive behaviours.

It's the availability and the ease.

In light of this, online bullying is becoming an addiction for some people, with social media providing a 24-hour free supply of material — all of it feeding into that bully's idea of blame. Blame is a useful way of considering why a workplace bully will target a person online, as well as in real life. Even if a bully is simply researching their target, or nursing their wrath, it is still unhealthy behaviour and is in effect digital stalking.

Everyone gets the concept of 'blame culture' — and they get the remedy, too. The opposite of 'blame culture' looks like this:

> "What can we do to help here? Instead of saying that this situation is someone's fault and focusing on that — let's take responsibility, understand our part in the problem, and move to a remedy that way."

Targets of bullying at work are however subject to the types of people who cannot help but react on their impulses, and although a bully may regret sending a message without either rethinking their position or considering the consequences — the damage remains done.

In terms of cyberbullying, we often see blame delivered outright in such ill-considered messages, which bullies then double down upon.

Sam Farley:

> "In the modern workplace, bullying is likely to take place to a greater extent through technology, and this makes bullying much harder to tackle for organisations, as it may be taking place outside of working hours on non-work media. Therefore, human resources practitioners will need to be proactive in developing processes for dealing with such scenarios."

This is what makes that spiky ball so relevant today, and so much harder to handle. It's because bullies in the 21st Century can reach their targets around the clock, and potentially do so anonymously. Enabling bullying to be a 24 / 7 undertaking has meant that there is no security for targets, even outside of work. It can be invasive, and for targets there is no escape, and it can be impossible to remove oneself from the line of fire. Lack of security doesn't even begin to cover it.

This is the biggest development in bullying as far as it persists at work in the Internet Age. There was a time when bullying could at least be said to stop when you crossed your front door — but not any longer.

Educator and therapist Gabriella Clarke of Mind Health Movement (mindhealthmovement.com) has experience of working with targets of online bullying. Her findings reflect that of the therapeutic community as a whole in identifying email as having its own special properties, which make it attractive to bullies.

"The difference I have noticed in recent years is that

> bullying is happening more over email and bullies are finding out more about their victims' personal lives via social media stalking," she says. "I think it depends on the environment, but in general I would say that tech-based bullying is slowly replacing 'in person' bullying behaviours, because it makes bullying easier."

The message is stark. A bully can reach their target at any time and by a variety of channels and methods. Their tools of hurt include:

Flaming — This is when people use deliberately offensive language or opinions in an attempt to rile targets, and cause or intensify arguments and fights. Perpetrators enjoy the reactions they provoke, including any signs of distress.

Exclusion — This is an extremely common bullying tool, used when someone is intentionally left out of a group or other form of engagement. Outside of a work context, this is a form of social bullying and it is common because it is so easy for those indulging in it to claim that no harm was meant, or that it was done by accident or in error.

Inappropriate Images — If you take a person's picture, you must have their permission, especially if it is going to be posted to the Internet. Taking an unwanted picture and circulating it without the subject's permission is a bullying behaviour — especially if you tag the picture, attempt to distribute it to a wider audience, or digitally alter it. A case of bullying in Scotland involved a woman who in 2010, complained of a racist and misogynistic culture in a government department, who was then taped to a chair, gagged and photographed by two male colleagues — 'as a warning to keep quiet.' (bbc.co.uk 23.05.2018).

Denigration — This is also common and is a form of 'bullying by memo'. It occurs when someone sends information about another person that is fake, damaging or untrue. You could liken it to a kind of online gossip, but such messages also include the kind of surprise texts and messages that targets receive from their bullies. A target can be sitting at home, free from the responsibilities of work — and yet they can still be reached — with the surprise factor only adding to the hurt. Such e-bullying also allows the possibility of others being copied in on mails. Magnifying the hurt.

One of the challenges of such forms of e-bullying is that the messages and actions are permanent and can be traced back to the individual from which they originated. You may think that people who bully might like to avoid leaving an e-trail of their actions — but they often don't think like that. Workplace bullying will always include an element of the bully shaming the target, and shaming messages tend to be held privately by targets. That is the self-evident nature of the messages, and they are often never shown to partners, spouses and friends, far less colleagues.

These messages, because they are digital, will never go away even when consigned to the trash. For a bullying individual, such messages are a permanent record not of their behaviour — but of their target's flaws and shortcomings.

It is this sense of justification that often marks bullies out. Targets know that an ongoing series of aggressions, sometimes punctuated with periods of calm, can make bullying virtually impossible to prove, even when it feels obvious to them. For targets, it will be tangible in their declining health and their loss in self-confidence. While one aggressive email or message does not automatically point to workplace bullying — a series of them over time certainly does.

We are all now potentially weaponised with technology, with laptops and phones which can be used for ill as well as they can for anything else. Mercifully, most of us adhere to agreed behaviours implicit in a workplace context. We don't terrorise by email, or take pictures without permission, seek to denigrate or humiliate others, rumour-monger, highlight inadequacies or consciously exclude others.

We choose not to wage cyber war and we resist inflicting pain and the option of being able to do so 24 / 7.

Sadly, not everyone does.

BULLIED? YOU TALKIN' TO ME?

So many manifestations of bullying are obvious. Physical bullying for example. An act of violence against another person is tangible and visible. It may even result in physical injury such as bruising, cuts or in extreme cases bloodshed.

In contrast, what is known as 'relational bullying' is far more subtle, consequently hard to detect and above all difficult to prove.

Relational bullying first emerges among young people before they have any meaningful experience of work. In many ways, schools are places where would-be relational bullies get to stress-test their techniques. They use these techniques to leverage power and always deploy them at the expense of another's social standing.

This might take the form of spreading malicious gossip to deliberately injure an individual and cause them distress. Other variants include breaking confidences; ensuring an individual is excluded from a group through sabotaging behaviour; encouraging the rest of the peer group to feel negatively towards an individual and more overtly indulging in a type of negative cheerleading.

Rumour. Exclusion. Betrayal. These are the tools of the relational bully. And all eminently exportable into adult life and the workplace.

Chantal Gautier, Chartered Psychologist, senior lecturer at a London-based university and author of *The Psychology of Work: Insights Into Successful Working Practices* (Kogan Page, 2016), believes that many of us absorb relational bullying into our day to day working lives and accept behaviours that in essence constitute bullying. She says:

> "I believe many don't realise they are being bullied, often because we do not know what constitutes bullying. We get used to certain things happening at work as 'normal' when they are not."

As much as anything else, it looks like our tolerances and expectations are crucial to any analysis of bullying. After all, if your need to keep your job is desperate and anchored by financial necessity or societal pressure, just how much are you prepared to put up with?

Let's look at the case of Alison and Diana as an example. Gender-wise relational bullying is more prevalent among women than men and this is because men are more used to outward physical bullying (a behaviour likely to have been established in an earlier educational setting) whereas women's more obvious default is covert bullying behaviour.

Alison doesn't like Diana and wants her gone from the workplace. Both work in an office setting with Alison enjoying slight seniority. Alison is sufficiently calculating to realise that a direct appeal to her boss to get rid of Diana won't play. So she resorts to covert bullying and has a clearly structured action plan in place. At what point would you check-out?

The campaign starts at a barely detectable level. Alison casually shares with two colleagues how she's concerned about Diana and how her personal life seems to be having a detrimental effect on her work. She is, of course, the first and only person to identify this. The seed has, however, been planted.

This escalates to Alison 'accidentally' forgetting to invite Diana to a work event, as part of her isolating and excluding campaign. This does not prove to be a one-off however, and Diana is systematically ignored.

Rumours are spread with Alison always being the source.

The gossip mongers are fed.

Alison then confronts Diana and makes it clear to her that she will only be satisfied once Diana has left her job. She conveys this in a one-to-one situation with no witnesses.

Diana is now delivered into a nightmarish work environment. Where malicious gossip and innuendo centres around her, where isolation is now part of her day to day experience and where her ability to concentrate on her job is impaired. Alison's plan is coming to fruition. She has managed to destabilise and distress her target to such an extent that Diana is now considering leaving.

Diana's work performance has certainly suffered in the process. Alison is then able to go to her boss and express her concerns about Diana and now has evidence that she is underperforming. Her wish fulfilment of a Diana-less workspace will soon be a reality.

This is not an unusual example of what some people might unhelpfully call 'workplace politics' but what may otherwise be called bullying. A staged, gradual escalation of behaviours tearing at the individual's sense of self, the way they are perceived and finally aggregated to the point where staying in that workplace is almost impossible.

The question is: how relevant is this for you? How far do you identify with Diana? And, if you do, do you treat this as the price of working in the 21st century?

Chantal Gautier does point out that in the UK, there is the Health And Safety at Work Act of 1974, which enshrines our protections under law when at work. The Act makes mention of 'proven harassment' with the crucial word there being 'proven'. Because relational bullying, as established in our case study, is hard to prove if it is not seen or heard, this, she believes, has a knock-on effect on the number of bullying cases bought forward.

Gautier defines relational bullying when the behaviour is repeated over time and with the intent to hurt an individual. Indirect bullying comes in many forms including: demeaning an individual; setting up an individual to fail; excluding them from essential information; excluding them socially; undermining them; overloading them with work; threatening their position by suggesting their job is in danger; and so on.

When asked how she feels society is doing in terms of bullying in the workplace Gautier is decidedly pessimistic:

> "Things have changed dramatically over the years. However, for most employers these days work is about getting the most out of employees and in many cases, there is little concern over how that is achieved. Employer demands mean there's literally no time to breathe."

She adds:

> "It is like being on a treadmill you have no control over; you can't adjust the speed settings. It brings to mind the image of the hamster on a wheel that cannot get off."

Indeed, in some ways, she feels employees are being 'suffocated'. How so? "I think specifically in terms of the way that employees are micromanaged." The implication is clear: if you are being micromanaged the suggestion may be that your employer or manager does not trust you. Absolutely every act or decision is analysed. The cumulative effect of this over years can turn the workplace into an unforgiving, brutal and spirit-sapping place to be. Contrast that with an environment where job fulfilment is the focus. Gautier argues:

> "Job satisfaction can be found today, and it is in environments which offer autonomy, freedom to make decisions, offer a sense of behavioural latitude and the freedom to be allowed to make mistakes. And a climate that instils kindness, care, authenticity and integrity."

These things, she says, "make people feel valued". And value and by extension a sense of belonging are, as we know, pivotal to a positive work experience. Flip them over and denigration and isolation heavily identify the DNA of BULLY, INC.

Micromanagement — when employees are subject to

obsessive levels of control — is an extremely common bullying tool, and not to be overlooked. Worse, micromanagement is usually justified with (faked) messages about improvement, or the furtherance of positive goals.

A controversial example of such micromanagement emerged in January 2020 and was covered by the BBC in the interview '*Firms urged to crack down on office football chat* (bbc.co.uk 27.01.20)' in which UK Chartered Management Institute Chief Executive Ann Francke argued that "A lot of women, in particular, feel left out," when men are talking about football and cricket in workplaces.

What is controversial about this is that it opens the door on companies dictating and being able to define what people talk about. Francke commented that: "They [meaning the above asserted 'a lot of women'] don't follow those sports and they don't like either being forced to talk about them or not being included." Aside from the simplistic assumption that all sports fans are men, this is an attitude typical of highly controlling micromanagement. It is in fact OK to not be included in something, and nobody has the right to control such a thing as conversation — with the obvious caveat concerning whether or not it is causing distress or breaching accepted behaviours. This is a great example of the potential evils of micromanagement — the ability to regulate other people's behaviour on the strength of weak or even false premises.

The question remains: having dissected relational bullying, does it have any role in your work life right now? And if so, is the price worth paying?

WHY THE WORK EQUATION DOESN'T WORK FOR LGBT+

For LGBT+ people the exertion of bullying behaviour by an individual or group also includes the added repressive dimension of being forced to stay silent about their sexuality. This is likely to be because the workplace is perceived — either as an environment as a whole or through the behaviours of individuals or groups within — to be unsafe.

Stonewall — the UK-based group campaigning for equality for the LGBT+ community — commissioned a survey in April 2018 titled *LGBT In Britain: Work* and found 35% of those polled were unwilling to share their sexuality at their place of work. For trans individuals the figure rose to 51% while for black and ethnic minority staff the figure was 42%.

These figures suggest a corporate smothering — a built-in discriminatory culture which marginalises the marginalised.

A joint report from Stonewall and the TUC (Trades Union Congress) titled *The Cost Of Being Out At Work* dug deep into LGBT+ bullying. Far from being vociferous in making others aware of bullying at work, there was a sense that LGBT+ workers were burnt out when it came to making official complaints and registering the fact that they had been bullied. Just over a third of those polled bothered to report their most recent experience of bullying to their employer, while barely one in eight reported to their company's HR department. Some 51% of all respondents admitted to being publicly 'out' at work, while this figure dropped to 36% for young people specifically. Some 27% who identified as bisexual opted not to share this with their colleagues.

Behind all these figures are individuals whose careers have been upended, diverted or even destroyed.

Former Chief Executive of Stonewall Ruth Hunt highlighted how eradicating these cultures is not only preferable on a humanitarian level but on an economic one too. She said: "Creating a workplace that accepts everyone isn't just the right thing to do, it makes good business sense. When staff feel comfortable and happy, they will perform much better than if they're having to hide who they are."

In the States GLAAD (Gay & Lesbian Alliance Against Defamation) reports similar figures with four out of ten LGBTQ workers identifying as being bullied. But — and this is astonishing — actual bullying in the workplace is not necessarily the first time LGBT workers encounter bullying or bigotry in a work context.

In Japan according to a survey conducted by Tokyo-based ReBit (dedicated to helping sexual minorities in their job hunting) some 40% of lesbian, gay and bisexual students admitted to 'uncomfortable experiences' during job interviews: all this prior to any active work experience. That figure rockets to 80% for transgender students.

Let's think about that for a moment. Statistically the survey — drawn on figures over a ten-year period — shows there are a significant number of environments that make no pretence to be anything other than hostile to the LGBT+ community.

That is to say that these companies are so maladjusted that they do not even bother with the pretence of being accepting of LGBT+ even at interview stage and thus have bigotry clearly embedded in their business DNA. Candidates also complained about the assumption being made that they were heterosexual, with 78% consciously hiding their LGBT+ identity.

With all the variants of bullying widely known and going on across all industries, LGBT+ workers are arguably more vulnerable than their heteronormative colleagues.

We invited LGBT+ workers to share their experiences of work in the UK and the responses were consistently depressing.

Allan, 23, an engineer based in Edinburgh, spoke of how he "chose to hide" his LGBT identity before being involuntarily outed when he was seen leaving a gay club in the city centre:

> "It was just bad timing. For me at least. Engineering is a very traditionally male vocation in both senses. It wasn't long before I found myself in trouble. It began with frequent suggestions I'd probably want to go and see the Lady Boys Of Bangkok (theatrical group) who were frequent visitors to the Edinburgh Festival.

> Flyers were left on my desk. I could see where it was all going and I decided to hand in my notice. Getting another job wasn't hard; it's a very specialist field. But that's not the point. I actually liked the work and until my outing I liked the people too. They had seemed nice."

Not everyone is so decisive or indeed has the freedom to be so. Josette, 31, worked in a retail environment where her choice of clothing caused her problems. "I've never been what you'd call a girlie girl; I am as I am. I don't make a big song and dance about being gay but, sure, people could put two and two together and come to that conclusion. My view has always been: so what?"

Josette describes how her day to day work life was made a misery:

> "From day one I felt my card was marked by two women. They acted as a unit really — so they'd criticise my clothes — one on one day, the other the next. It felt like a military assault. They were obsessed with my Doc Martens when they were staggering around in heels. I tried to rise above it. Then one night I bumped into them on the way home. And to anyone else it must have seemed like a normal conversation. But it really wasn't. They promised to keep making my life miserable. They also made it very clear they knew how far they could go. So, one said — and I'm still haunted by these words: We'll never hit you or anything physical. But we will f*** with your head and turn everyone against you."

Karen Beardsell is Director of HR at Stonewall and if there's a workplace template worth looking at in an LGBT+ context then it's there. Karen outlined to website theHRdirector.com how she approached her role within Stonewall when she took over.

> "Stonewall had devised a new vision of 'acceptance without exception', a world where everyone is free to be themselves. In order to achieve this, it was important to restructure the organisation, to ensure that individuals and teams were best placed to affect change in their specific roles. The team, our Staff Consultative Group, went on to help us develop the values that would truly belong to us and reflect what Stonewall now represented and was all about. One of the first objectives was to change the dress code, which was gendered, and amend this to be inclusive of non-binary and gender-nonconforming members of staff. The restructured policies produced a cultural change within the organisation, and increased staff satisfaction across all areas of their working lives, whether that involved feeling proud to work for Stonewall or being valued by managers. Importantly, we want all individuals, staff or otherwise, to think that this is an organisation for them. Which is as it should be, of course. However, the reality is rarely that and Stonewall – given its remit and raison d'etre must be considered exceptional."

The reality is this: if a workplace has an inbuilt tendency towards allowing a hostile environment to ferment, then statistically it is LGBT+ individuals who are more likely to suffer, whether it's by basic denial of who they are and how they identify all the way through to verbal or cyber abuse and indeed physical assault.

THE USES OF TRUTH

From playground to parliament and including every family and workspace in between, bullying is defined the same way: it is a continuing offensive by one person against another, or a group of others.

As bullying behaviours are never right, there have to be reasons why bullying individuals are therefore able to prolong their behaviours and not only repeat them — but get away with them.

One of the less obvious ways in which they can achieve this is by their use of certain truths. If you are a target, there will be truths about yourself that will have played a part in your being bullied.

This is not because you are a 'bully-magnet' or because of any specific character traits you may have been told you have. It is down to truths. There is no such thing as a 'bully-magnet'. It's like saying that dog dirt is automatically attracted to your shoes. It's an inversion of the facts and a mentality that needs to be challenged. There is no harm, in asking "what part of this problem do I own?" — but we are still talking about behaviours which may be good and right, or which may be wrong and harmful.

Even Lynne Curry, author of *Solutions and Beating the Workplace Bully* says that it is possible to 'magnetize' bullies (Anchorage Daily News 24.09.2019). Although she has carefully phrased this concept in the passive mode — i.e. one person's behaviour can serve to attract negative bullying behaviour so the 'magnetism' is not an active aspect of a target's personality — Lynne Curry is sure that there are still certain types of people who are more at risk:

> "Bullies operate with risk / benefit radar, zeroing in on individuals they consider easy prey. Do you turn yourself inside out to avoid conflict or making someone else mad? Do others know you won't confront them if they tread on you? Bullies eat nice people alive."

On some levels this may be right, but my experience and research oblige me to strongly disagree. I disagree because anyone can be bullied by another person, and anyone can resort to bullying behaviour. The failure very often lies in acknowledgement. We need to know what those bullying behaviours are because some situations at work — such as underperformance — are turned into bullying scenarios when they need not be. A supervisor or colleague should tell you only in a managed situation that your work has fallen short. When that information or belief is used against you in any way, that is bullying behaviour.

People prone to bullying behaviours undoubtedly use the perceived or real faults and errors of those they target as a propellant. Some individuals prone to bullying behaviours 'save up' the mistakes of their targets and deliver them in one surprise slap. Others will devise tactics specific to the conditions of their own particular workplace. Because we all make mistakes, we can all be bullied for them.

Bullying can be displayed by either commission — an active event such as a temper tantrum — or by omission — leaving someone out, ignoring them, or otherwise cutting the oxygen supply to their self-confidence:

> "I was in a meeting and I revealed some private information about one of my staff, their salary in fact, in front of an external person. This was a stupid mistake. The employee did the right thing and told another manager what I'd done but that other manager never mentioned it to me. I noticed she did this more than once. She saved up my mistakes. Then she would drop them when it suited her. I hadn't realised what I'd done so I could never apologise or make things right. In keeping my mistake secret, that other manager also walked over the feelings of the member of staff, basically using him as a tool to her bullying. She told me about what I'd done in an email ten months later! She used that incident to try and turn him against me. She did this several times and with different people. It was a pattern."
> (Paul, 39, Retail)

It's a fact of life that mistakes will be made, and it is a fact of bullying that mistakes will be used as ammunition. Bullying individuals know that if a target isn't aware they have done something wrong, or are short of information in any way, then that target cannot make amends. In the above case, the behaviour belonged 100% to the bully, and it was deliberate.

The effect of this bullying behaviour in this case was that the target's mistakes were amplified. This is an example of bullying by omission, which is generally subtler than bullying by commission, for example carried out by someone who openly insults another person, or shouts at them etc.

We cannot in any fair sense legislate for such omission, yet we can still see it happening. It is undermining — it creates conflict — it removes responsibility — it isolates and excludes — it is inconsistent — and it is a withholding of recognition as much as it is a withholding of information. It is bullying behaviour.

One suggestion for breaking this cycle is that we model imperfection. Modelling imperfection means that instead of covering up our mistakes, we can use negative situations as an opportunity. Covering up mistakes, might mean for example:

- Pretending the mistakes aren't happening or real;
- Doubling down on mistakes;
- Blaming others, or circumstances.

To make matters worse, it is usually the case that if a person is being bullied, they will make mistakes and those mistakes will be the subject of much closer scrutiny, certainly by a bully, and possibly by others.

Those who can hold up their hands to acknowledge mistakes, however, can find a way through, usually with the help of other people. What should have happened in the above case is obvious. The manager who made the mistake should have been told and allowed to make amends. It is entirely possible that staff would have considered this man to have been a 'bad manager', but I do not think they would ever know this had they not been able to see how he dealt with his mistakes. As it was, the mistake was used against this manager in an instance of workplace bullying.

In role-modelling imperfection, we can show that mistakes will not be punished, that mistakes are not the end of the world, that we are all capable of mistakes, and that errors of judgement can be worked with.

For targets of bullying, the fear of failure is a regular trigger, and mistakes are always intensified. This does not need to be the case. Some modern companies, exampled in a later chapter by the high-street handmade cosmetics company Lush, have chosen to operate with the attitude that staff and managers have a 'right to make mistakes'.

As a company policy this works wonders. For a start — as the old saw reminds us — to err is human. We could add to this that to manage errors by anger or through shaming is bullying behaviour! This is a million miles away from being a so-called 'bully magnet' — a person who is 'more likely to be bullied' for a certain characteristic or habit.

First, a magnet can change, and I would suggest to the magnet that there is an inherent contradiction in the description it gives of itself. I would ask people who believe they are bully magnets to examine their thinking closely! Consider the words of therapist Mary O'Neill, who has a Master's degree which explores the dynamics of workplace bullying:

"Targets of bullying tend to blame or question

> themselves and so tend to feel not OK while everyone else is OK. This creates a perfect foil for the bully who is looking to blame someone. And so, they fall into the trap of letting themselves be blamed. When people are bullied, they feel worthless and every client I have worked with has said they lose confidence in themselves. They are so used to someone belittling them or criticising them that they end up questioning everything, including their own sanity."

It is true that shy people, people who are different, and those who don't conform to gender norms can find themselves as the targets of intimidation and harassment. These and others suffer constant bullying, because there is an element of being 'othered' in bullying.

Bullying is a behavioural issue and an organisational issue. This means that the propensity to be bullied is not something that could be said to be inherent in any person or type of person, even if these individuals are in some way compromised or unable to defend themselves.

Mary O' Neill continues:

> "It's not that targets can't stand up for themselves. It's just that to do so would mean disciplinary procedures so they sit on this anger and it festers. When a personality study says targets of bullying are less agreeable and more neurotic, they may be measuring this after bullying has gone on for months or years and so these personality traits are impacted by the bullying."

The essence of othering is revealed in concept called the 'OK Corral' which is developed from a therapeutic method called Transactional Analysis.

TA, as it is called, is a flexible therapy which styles our behaviours during interactions into the categories of Adult, Parent and Child, a method of analysis which allows us to place actions and situations in light of these suggested relationships.

The concepts of TA, as Mary O'Neill explains it, contain "no psychobabble" — and can provide a useful set of tools to help us manage our lives. The 'OK Corral' theory states that we strive to feel respectful and valuing about ourselves, while we hope at the same time to feel respectful and valuing towards others. You could call this position I'm OK / You're OK.

However, when we are stressed, we move to other positions and those who tend to gravitate to an I'm OK / You're not OK position do so because they believe they haven't done anything wrong. This is however a position with potential for bullying.

Daily examples of this might include eye-rolling, which is a typical sign that somebody has become a problem to someone else. If you watch a bullying person in conversation with someone they strongly disagree with, you'll see them check out of the conversation, usually with something like eye-rolling. Eye-rolling is one of the more obvious but also widely ignored bullying behaviours in our workplaces. Eye-rollers everywhere are in effect saying: "I have had enough of this conversation. This person is a problem for me and is the issue here. I am now treating this person as 'not OK'". The reason this is moving into bullying behaviour is because the issue under discussion has ceased to be the focal point for one person. The 'other' has become the problem.

This does not enlighten us about the personality of the target, but it does allow targets to understand why it was they who suffered. To say that the target is the one with the problem is a highly blaming position, and it most clearly demonstrates the distinction between who is a target and who is a bully.

The 'You're not OK' attitude is often associated with people who lack insight into their actions, who are in effect people who cannot bear to be seen as not OK. This brings them to bullying behaviour when they fail to achieve a goal and state that a situation is someone else's fault. That situation is a bullying fundamental — a bully will be someone who is unable to bear the possibility of their being 'not OK'.

Bullies at work may be motivated by these attitudes, and although the personality of the target may be a deciding factor, essentially the target still has something a bully wants. While bullying behaviour may not be motivated by prejudice, it will invariably involve the target 'being othered'. Prejudice may be a tool that bullies use, but prejudice is not always the purpose bullying behaviour. The purpose of bullying is to make the bully's narrative 'the truth', and that can mean amplifying the mistakes of their target. The best way to do that is through shame.

This combative and threatening auto-reaction to errors at work is trying for targets, but it is a hallmark of bullying behaviour. Targets of bullying come to understand that the bullying behaviour is always personal and intended to repeatedly hurt. The same is true Paul (page 71):

• Mistakes which he may have made were treated as evidence of his unsuitability not just as a worker, but as a person, and —

• This message was fed back to him in private emails, which informed him that everybody agreed with his bully's view, even though this was not true.

As a manager who preferred to 'own' his mistakes by identifying them and progressing to correct them, this retail manager therefore found himself more significantly abused for his errors than the situation merited.

Being a perfectionist is not as healthy an option as trying to be yourself and that is one of the reasons we can chose to 'model imperfection' when it occurs. It's also one of the reasons that apparently low-level bullying behaviour such as blaming, when carried out over time, leads to mental health problems. If you are trying to deal with that level of criticism, the weight will take its toll.

There is never any harm in the truth and there is no shame in making mistakes. The costs of mistakes are more than just economic, and everyone likes to have a good reputation. If you are making mistakes at work, this will not be a comfortable time, and if you are making mistakes because of a bully, such mistakes may become more numerous and eat at your self-confidence.

If for some reason you really are poor at your job, then you will be obliged to give that some consideration, but only if it is addressed in an arranged or team-meeting-style of environment.

Indeed — the circumstances of such a meeting are

nothing less than a safe environment where such difficult assertions may be made because there is no opportunity for anything other than civility in dealing with them.

However, mistakes can be privately used by a bully to make that bully's narrative 'the truth'.

The paradigm of the I'm OK / You're Not OK situation therefore explains how a fear becomes a truth to a target, and how that truth will be made poisonous by a bully.

There is only one way to deal with grievance however and that is civility. The truth is an impossibly hard entity when delivered with the intention of hurt, and this is one of the ways in which bullying replays and recurs in the minds of targets — and for a long time.

It's called 'weaponizing', and it works because of the truth. It is the truth that keeps targets awake at night and it is the truth that causes them lasting psychological damage.

If you are still thinking of your bullying incident years after it has happened — that may be the truth replaying like a corrupted computer file in your mind. It is often the case that such true facts about ourselves are used against us — that we are sensitive as an example — that we made a mistake as an example — that we are or were not very good at your job at a certain time — as an example. These are examples of truths which could cause a person shame, even though that shame stems from the moment when the bully made them harmful.

When targets leave their workplaces because of bullying, they do so in theory of their own free will. Later however, when their health has improved, targets will go through a process of assessing everything that has been said and done to try and see if they can in any way reclaim their dignity from what has been a shaming experience. Often, they will see that little of what has been said is true.

Awareness of this hasn't done much to alleviate workplace bullying. Although bystanders can move on from incidents of bullying at work fairly quickly, targets do not move on so fast. Targets in fact very often leave their place of work, and leave friends, a career, or even a business behind. "More than a third of people who report bullying leave their job." (agencycentral.co.uk). If that statistic is valid, then stated in real terms, the costs are massive. If, as the TUC states, a third of people are bullied at work (tuc.org.uk 16.11.2019) and a third of those thereafter leave their jobs, then the damage we are talking about is extensive. It is so extensive in fact, that a great many of us must be condoning it.

Targets may leave workplaces over situations which they did not initiate, even if the situation arose from their own mistakes or their own lack of suitability. Neither of these factors are grounds for bullying, of course, but they do explain why bullying behaviour goes unchecked and why so many of us appear to condone it. The great questions regarding bullying behaviour are not in fact why people bully each other, but why the rest of us allow it happen. In condoning bullying then, we must therefore be invoking what we believe are truths, such as the belief that there are such things as 'bully magnets'. Often people are bullied out of jobs for personal reasons, and sometimes the reasons are operational and financial — all convenient truths by which we condone these behaviours.

Truths however, can always be dealt with civilly, and should never be weaponized and made harmful. Bullying behaviour can start small, and the temptation may be to let the small sins slide and to wait for larger and more obvious offences to be committed. But as with everything else in the world of workplace bullying, being aware of these behaviours around us is a huge help, and will allow any of us to see how such seemingly small incidents and interpersonal actions can lead to weaponizing. If we are aware of such weaponizing, even on a low level, we will be able to stop it in its tracks, either by modelling imperfection, if that works for us, or by recourse to a company's values.

Bullying can start small and it probably often does — yet simple things like failing to give constructive feedback or failing to deliver praise — like failing to give support — like minimising people in your language (eg: saying "you're far too sensitive") — and spreading gossip — all of these omissions will serve to undermine another person and induce anxiety.

These are the uses of truth. Often a bully at work will concentrate on these psychological elements and use them as tools to get their way. What that usually means for the target, sadly, is a slow decline in their mental health, and finally their self-imposed removal from the workplace.

BULLYING AND MENTAL HEALTH

Bullying is a health issue. I should really start every chapter with that reminder! Perhaps there has been a tendency in the past to consider workplace bullying as a conflict between individuals — but that's in the past and it's history. It's an out of date opinion and as dead as a discarded glove puppet.

The reason we know that bullying is a health issue is because mediators cannot help. In an instance of workplace bullying the target is already hurt — already compromised — already impaired. In many cases, by the time it comes to the attention of others in the workplace, the target is already ill, or about to become so.

Arbitration can begin when bullying behaviours are identified, but a lot of bullying can have flowed under the bridge before that happens, and significant damage can already have been done. ACAS are an example of a service in the UK which offer to help rebuild work relations although this can only happen if your workplace is willing to acknowledge mistreatment in the first place and isolate the behaviours of a bully. In the US, conventional litigation is more common, although there is a growing body of methods of Alternative Dispute Resolutions (ADRs). The title still however suggest that bullying is a 'dispute' — which it categorically is not.

There is a difference between mediation and the work of mediators, and the necessary rebuilding of work relations after or during a case of workplace bullying. A mediator cannot help a target of bullying because bullying is based on mistreatment for which there is no honest justification.

Writer and conflict expert Sarah Hussain says that offering mediation in a case of bullying is "like asking a victim of violence to discuss the issue with their attacker." And she is absolutely right. A bully will offer excuses for their behaviour, generally in the form of the same attacks they have been making on their target all along. They have made the other person the issue, and in doing so have caused a significant mental health risk.

Sarah Hussain goes on to explain that in workplaces which routinely offer mediation in dealing with bullying, "regardless of the outcome, there are no consequences for the bully and no real answers for the complainant."

Putting this simply, a mediator can only help when two people have opposing views. A mediator may be helpful after workplace bullying has been resolved, and such a mediator might address the challenges of a target returning to work.

However — bullying is a systematic and interpersonal campaign of mistreatment that has nothing in common with conflict. A conflict is a difference of opinion that has gone out of control, whereas bullying has one person targeting another in order to damage their career, their health, their family cohesion and their standing in the workplace. Conflict between two equally powered parties is not bullying. It's a different planet in a different universe.

I stress this because often bullying is perceived by bystanders as a conflict — and that is a huge boost for the bully. Take an example of cyberbullying in which, let's imagine someone is sending messages to another person stating that they are overweight. Would a mediator really look at that situation and suggest to the target that if they lose weight, then they are likely to receive less of these messages? Of course not. What a third party can and must focus on is the emotional abuse — which are the actions of the bully.

A bully at work will therefore present their activity as if it were a conflict of opinion, personality or interest. But there is a difference. It is the bully's unwillingness to listen that breaks the model. With a bully at work it is usually a case of 'take it or leave it' when it comes to their targets, who are typically not in a position to challenge the options and so must accept the bully's decision or suffer negative consequences. These consequences will amount to more bullying behaviours — the arms folded attitude — the lack of communication — the back-biting — the criticism — the manoeuvring — and everything else that bullies have in their armoury. Mediation is never going to work in cases of emotional abuse, because even if the bully thinks of the situation as a clash or a conflict — it is not.

Someone I spoke to tactfully referred to a situation at their work as involving a person leaving amid 'shades of bullying'. This is a useful bystander phrase because it tones down the real accusation. 'Shades of bullying' also points directly into the massive grey areas in which bullies operate.

Because bullying behaviours often appear on a 'take it or leave it' basis, the target holds their own until they become ill, or start to feel too much pressure. If targets don't like their jobs to begin with, they will maybe move on amid what bystanders may call 'shades of bullying'.

If targets enjoy their jobs or need the job for another reason, they will be hard to shift, and this is when their health can go into decline.

Targets report the same thing — the fundamental responses to bullying are feelings of vulnerability, guilt and isolation. The targets of bullying worry about whether they are overreacting to a situation and they can become paranoid, or suspicious when they have no call to. Generally, targets of bullying are concerned that they have brought this trouble upon themselves — all feelings and symptoms which are similar to those reported by sufferers of mental ill-health.

What is the difference then between being the target of bullying behaviour and suffering poor mental health? Substantially none.

> "After being bullied, and then becoming ill, and had my mental health made the subject of far too many conversations, some of which I am sure I wasn't even party to, I realised I had to leave immediately. The discussion of my capability at my job never ceased once it had begun. On the occasions when I gave in and let this certain person have their way, the same pattern only resurfaced around another issue — and so the downward spiral progressed. What happened to me wasn't unique, either, I could also see it going on with other people. I was not the only person to just leave suddenly like that." (Richard, 49, e-commerce start-up)

For the most part, bullies attack and see the response. Thereafter it is the response that is made into the issue and not the initial attack. So — for example — the target will be considered as a 'difficult employee' if they cannot handle 'frank criticism' — and in this and other examples, a bully may keep attacking until they get the response they want.

I wonder if you can see where this is going? There are many physical and mental symptoms which can and do result from bullying, and the most common of these are as follows. The source is medicine.net, although these symptoms are consistent across all expert health sites:

- High blood pressure
- Anxiety (may include panic attacks)
- Sleep disruption
- Loss of concentration
- Headaches
- Mood swings
- Stress disorder
- Disordered eating
- Clinical depression
- Nausea
- Feeling uncoordinated
- Rapid breathing
- Uncontrolled crying

These are just some of the bodily and mental symptoms of bullying. They are common symptoms which are typically reported by people who have been targeted by any of many possible emotional abuses at work.

These are also symptoms which are entirely consistent with many general and specific mental health concerns, yet when targets of bullying go to their doctor, it is unlikely that they will receive a diagnosis of 'bullying'. A person may receive a diagnosis like 'anxiety' or 'depression', or variations thereof.

The important corollary here is that targets of workplace bullying are often absent from work with sicknesses which have their origin in the workplace — their origin in bullying.

I mention this as something to be aware of, whoever you are. People are made ill by bullying. Thereafter, it is typical bullying behaviour for someone to identify a target as unfit, with a kind of shoulder-shrugging confidence.

In clinical cases of depression, it is not easy to distinguish between life events that may have caused a complaint and those events which may have been the result of the complaint. What we can be sure of however is that if we are in the territory of bullying, we will almost certainly be in the territory of mental health.

The reverse is of course not true. Mental health disorders and malaises linked to work, do not automatically point to bullying. But if we are discussing bullying, we will almost certainly also be talking about mental health.

To unpick these health concerns and find out if they have been established in the workplace, it helps targets if they can speak to people that are not in any way associated with their job. Targets are advised to place their confidence in people they can trust outside of their work — people that are able to confirm to them the changes that have occurred in their health — those also who may be willing to listen to why these changes have occurred.

In the meantime, do not lose sight of the fact that the symptoms of bullying are consistent with those of a range of other ailments. If you are targeted by bullying behaviour, seek help in coping with that situation but also work on improving your health as you do so. In treating illnesses related to workplace bullying, the sooner the issue can be addressed the better. For this reason, professional counselling or therapy can be useful. Going to a therapist or seeking similar help may be a daunting step, but it shouldn't be. Most people have no fear about going to the doctor for physical ailments, and yet if you look at the symptoms above — all consistent with indications of workplace bullying — you'll see that all of those so-called 'mental' symptoms are all also physical to varying degrees.

Targets of bullying however do not always seek medical help when it is needed. This might be because they feel shame, or they might not recognise the connection between their bullying experiences and their health.

> "For the target, being shamed is a humiliating experience as they are systematically told and reminded that their worth as a human is not valued. Just as the aggressors make it clear they are unwanted and not valued, the target of bullying feels, on some level, that they must be what they are viewed as." (Janice Harper Ph.D. *Beyond Bullying*)

This downturn in health cannot happen overnight. For this process to be fulfilled, it needs to happen over a period of time, and be masterminded — consciously or not — by a bullying individual. This can begin with something simple like exclusion, back-biting, unconstructive criticism and other 'shades' of bullying behaviour.

In the meantime, don't ever be told that bullying is a matter of conflict or that it is a personality clash.

Sometimes people's behaviour turns unprofessional because they have fallen out with each other, but this is different from targeting. It takes two people to have a fight, and both of them need to be fighting. If a bully targets another person, they might like to present it as a fight for the benefit of bystanders, because it will help their campaign. But bullying is not a matter of conflict.

This idea that bullying is a conflict or a clash of personalities is always worth challenging. In fact, treat the statement as the red flag it is. Often, when there is little hard evidence of a bullying campaign, and when facts are observed in 'shades' or deliberately muddied, you can simply tell that a bully has been at work by the destruction they have wrought upon the health of their targets.

The suggestion that the problem is somehow the target themselves, is a warning sign that a bully is at work.

THE AMBUSH MEETING

I attended a meeting this morning. Present were some people from my company and the representative of another company. It went well. We all got something from the meeting and moved forward towards our respective and shared aims. This was the desired result of the meeting — but the bully sometimes has meetings with you that aren't like this.

It is important to differentiate between those who have the right intentions and may have the wrong methodology or may be ill-equipped for a task or a role — and those who have intentions that they may not even be clear about themselves. Often, we know a bully by their results — a targeted person leaving their job; or a targeted person who was once well and doing a good job, transformed into someone who is unwell and unable to work. In what sense are we saying these things are intentional on the part of a bully?

The intentions of bullying individuals are rooted in areas far from the workplace and perhaps also far back in time, potentially in the bully's parental home. These intentions are somehow present in bullying behaviour but as so much bullying is relational, and in some senses 'undercover', these intentions are not always going to be clear. Even though you may have met a workplace bully, you cannot be expected to know them, which is why we focus for the most part on their behaviour. Just about all bullying that goes on in the home happens in private, and so cannot be said to be observable to bystanders in the same way that mistreatment at work will be. As for a bully's intentions, these are a strictly private matter, and may only become apparent in private situations. The rules of the household are so different to the rules of the workplace and so is the assumed privacy. Privacy and a person's dark intentions go hand in hand, however. This means that a target will only ever be shown the dark intentions of the bully in a situation where there is absolute privacy. This is why a target should never go unprepared into a one-to-one meeting with someone who has a potential for bullying behaviour. This is not always practical, but it is still a golden rule.

The name for this type of meeting is the 'ambush meeting' and the fundamentals are described by the website know-bull.com:

> "Up until now, you may not have even realised you were the target of a workplace bully. Many people don't — they just put this kind of workplace abuse down the rigours of working with a 'demanding' person. If that's the case, then this meeting is going to be one of the worst shocks of your life."

Many of the normal rules of communication are up for grabs in this type of one-to-one meeting, because everything is your word against mine. The ambush meeting is the have-it-all moment for the bully, and this is why it is essential to be aware of what ambush meetings are and how they happen. You might not know that you are being bullied at work, although you may have suspicions. But if you really are being bullied there will almost certainly come a time when such an ambush meeting happens, and so knowing about what to expect in advance can be life-saving.

Even the most effective of us cannot work hard enough, nor well enough, for a bully. Bullying individuals will always argue that your results aren't up to scratch and this will become more apparent when you get behind closed doors with them. You'll know that you're in an ambush meeting, because you will be asked to justify yourself.

There are healthy steps you can take to prepare for the possibility of an ambush meeting. First, if you think that there is any risk of bullying behaviour taking place, ask if the meeting can happen in the open, perhaps in a shared workspace or a public venue. You can also do your best to invite another person to the meeting, although this won't always be appropriate. If you ask someone to attend on this basis, do not be afraid to let them know that you feel under threat.

When you find yourself in such an ambush meeting, it is important to keep calm. There are two types of ambush meeting, one in which bureaucratic or procedural processes will be used to remove a person; and there are meetings in which a person will receive emotional abuse. Presumably there can be meetings which are both, but it is important that in the case of the second one, that targets are able to get up and leave, and thereby remove themselves from the possibility of more hurt.

Emotional abuse in ambush meetings can range from delivering threats and insults to other forms of intimidation. It can be wordless in the form of overbearing body language, or 'the silent treatment', and it can be directed not at you — but at inanimate objects, either thrown or kicked around. 'Storming out' is also emotional abuse. 'Storming out' and other tantrum-style activity is bullying behaviour because it sends the message that you are refusing to communicate, and that other people are the problem — not you. People who 'storm out' are trying to dictate when a meeting is over, but they are doing so in the most embarrassing way. People who 'storm out' have reached the end of their possibilities as communicators, and so they employ the dramatic exit as a method of bullying. Thus, be reminded that 'storming out' and directing violence against inanimate objects, including throwing things, is bullying behaviour, and is not acceptable at work.

Trying to remain calm and collected while this is going on might seem like a reasonable response, but it doesn't in reality help. Worse than this, the targets of ambush meetings generally stay in such meetings far too long. That is, they fail to get up and leave. Being prepared to leave an ambush meeting is a valuable asset. It is completely different from storming out and it can happen in numerous ways — so long as we can describe it as politely leaving.

When we suffer any type of abuse at all, including the verbal abuse we may receive in such a meeting, there are some definite behavioural and physiological follow-ons. If we feel ourselves becoming a victim, for example, when this happens, we will start to behave like a victim and that will include a victim communication style which will extend outside of work. If unchecked, 'victim-thinking' will continue with us even when we are alone.

Further, permitting the abuse also rewards the bully. It only needs to happen once. Allowing a co-worker to get away with emotionally abusive tactics even one time, tells them that it works — and this is why when this happens to any of us, we must remove ourselves, and at the first opportunity. It should be you as the target that is the one that establishes that enough is enough — not them. This is why people who become aggressive, for example, during difficult conversations, behave the way they do. They do it because they have got away with it previously. If a co-worker is shutting someone down by using fear or by other means, they are bullying that other person, and we know it's bullying because it is not happening by mutual consent.

One way to leave such a situation in a healthy manner, might be what communication trainer Dan O' Connor calls the Redirect With Assumptions. This doesn't mean shouting in someone's face and then storming off. It's just the opposite. What it means is saying something like: "I can see this is isn't working and so I am going to leave now." — or any of several variations thereof.

The Redirect With Assumptions can then come into play along the following lines:

"When you're ready to …" (Redirect)
"Then I will be ready to …" (Assumption)

So I might therefore say something like this to someone

who is bullying me: "When you're ready to continue this conversation without resorting to (and then I might mention a bullying behaviour) — then I will be ready to find a solution" — or whatever it may be.

This is easier said than done, especially considering the surprise factor — as typified in the word 'ambush'. But that is why this kind of thinking doesn't hurt, even when we are not being bullied.

In therapeutic work, it is often considered that there is a fight, flight or freeze response to crisis, and while none of these are the 'right' course of action, they are simply listed as the three main responses a person will resort to when experiencing a sudden attack or similar provocation. The rationale behind fight, flight or freeze is that you will not know in advance which one you will do.

We can be prepared however and armed with good measure. We must always remember in ambush meetings, for example, never to try and refute the claims being made against us. These will be claims that were prepared in advance and there is also a strong possibility that there will be too many of them to deal with, and that they will be falling with the rapidity of machine gun fire. Countering the criticism will be like trying to catch those machine gun bullets, and you will fail to argue your case in the most painful way.

If you suspect that an ambush meeting might be coming and you cannot avoid it, then one thing to remember is to maintain your silence, because your silence is your dignity. The goal of the typical ambush meeting is to have you leave the company — that is to voluntarily resign — although I say 'voluntarily' advisedly. You are still being forced out. It is what has been called a 'constructive dismissal' and when used at a formal level, may involve something like an 'improvement plan' being presented to you — something that says you have a certain amount of time to improve your performance, or else you will be released.

You should never under any circumstances freely sign such a document — and if you find yourself signing such a thing under threat, then score out the word 'Signature' and replace it with the words 'Signed Under Protest' or 'Forced To Sign' — or something similar. If you're presented with such a document, try and remember that you are not obliged to sign it and that you will have other options.

Being presented with such a document is in fact a virtual substantiation of bullying behaviour.

Those who have signed such documents will corroborate this. They know already that if you ever do sign such an agreement you will be guaranteeing that the bullying behaviour will increase — just as if you fail to control the outcome of the ambush meeting, the same can be said — the bullying will increase. The aim of the ambush meeting is to get you to leave the workplace and if it can be achieved with you doing so of your own volition, then all the better.

It's tough to accept, but once the ambush meeting has occurred you might have to start looking for another job.

That's not easy to hear, especially if you like your job. But this is the extremity of the process and it's why the bullying behaviour of some people is life-altering for others.

One of the best pieces of advice a target of bullying can take is that they be 100% reasonable. Targets are advised to avoid one-to-one meetings for the same reason, because that is where the worst provocations occur. If you suspect you are being bullied, then your next meeting could be that ambush meeting, and nothing about it is going to be fair.

Remember that your actions and words must be beyond reproach and justifiable. If you are ambushed don't do or say anything that you would not wish to repeat in public — because your bully will. If you are provoked and make an unhealthy or negative response, then that response will be made the issue. And if you manage to get out such an ambush meeting with some dignity, do not go back to that person to continue the conversation — wait until they come to you. This is the purpose of the Redirect With Assumptions.

If you are being bullied at work, then an ambush meeting is certainly going to come at some point and you can at least be ready.

Otherwise, it's going to be like a trap shutting fast around you — not fair I know — but your health is important — it's even more important than your job.

Find those around you who will support you and do so quickly. One of the keys to minimising any trauma is to catch the sufferer early — the earlier the better.

This will help you make that moral acknowledgement that you need: I was bullied and it was not acceptable.

I WAS BULLIED AND IT WAS NOT ACCEPTABLE

Holding its own as bravely as it can in the middle of the word 'intimidation' — sits the word 'timid'.

All of us have an insecure side, and in fact insecurity can be pronounced in bullies — even if it is hidden behind a hard-bitten front. It's maybe for that reason that some bullies don't like timid people. It's almost as if a timid person is publicly acknowledging their insecurity by not speaking up, by fearing confrontation and keeping themselves to themselves.

Certainly, shyness is not to be considered by anybody as a negative. Timid people have their reasons and timid people must go to work as well. Traditional advice for timid people is that they should be more assertive but I have to confess that I admire people who don't like being shouted at in anger — I see that as a positive and I do not think it should be they who changes. If someone shouts at me in anger I don't feel there is a need for me to shout back. It's painful to let workplace shouters treat other people like this, but their anger is always their problem and should never be made anybody else's.

For some people, being assertive is often also the wrong thing to do. It might be somebody's first day of being assertive in a long time and they may be asserting them self before someone who has had daily practice in being a domineering and self-willed dragon for years.

There is a relationship between bullying behaviour and shyness, but it isn't direct. One way to think of it is in reverse. That is to say that the quality of shyness is something that is sometimes actually desirable to a bullying individual. It's as if the bullying individual is seeing something they can never have — like a graceful shoe that will never fit on a great clawed foot.

Although shy people may feel discomfort in social or working situations, it may actually suit them, and is at the same time perfectly acceptable, and not a cause for criticism. Some workplaces can be fairly shouty, and even if temper tantrums and yelling are not a daily or weekly event, such emotional outbursts can become common enough to be accepted as a fact of life. If that has happened in your workplace, your workplace has already shifted into the bully-zone.

If you have had experience of someone who is regularly angry with others, or who shouts at people or talks over them, you may already have spotted that individuals who behave like this do what they can to normalise it. Shouters may say things, for example, to the effect that raising of the voice is 'normal' and sometimes 'needed'. Places where this happens can be oppressive to work in and it doesn't matter how it is couched, it is still a dispiriting thing to witness. It is a culture of what could only be described at the very philosophical best as 'acceptable levels of shouting' or 'justifiable yelling at others' or 'excusable rude responses' — amazing phrases that I have genuinely come across as justifications for bad behaviour. Shouting however is for some people intolerable and upsetting, and yet it can still quite easily become a culture at work.

If you are in one of these workplaces where shouting in anger is tolerated, then you already have a problem. We must unanimously let the shouters know that they cannot get away with it. As with all bullying behaviours, if somebody gets away with such abuse once, they will continue to do so.

This is the reward that bullies get and by doing nothing about it, the rest of us hand it to them. And so this is how even one or two unacknowledged and unchallenged displays of aggression can lead to a big old angry mess.

Working with such insights, we can see how a set of values will help each individual prosper, as well as the company. A set of values means that any behaviour can be challenged and at any time, even if bullying behaviours have become embedded. Values will root this out and cause everyone to pay attention.

Clarifying what your values are will help you in numerous ways, especially if you write them down and refer to them often. A good place to write them down may be on your social media profile. Writing your values on a social media profile will mean that you are not only aware of your values, but that you are proud of them. You will be proud of your values because once they are stated they will start to work for you.

Just how does that operate in the real world, however?

Let's say that my stated personal values are as follows — that I aspire to fun — safety — and creativity. I can use these values for a multitude of purposes, but here are some working examples:

- I know that when an aspect of my life, whether work or relationship, stops being fun, safe or creative, then I should address the issue.

- Others know that in working with me, they can expect me to be fun, safe and creative. If I am not working to these values, then others who are working with me have grounds to open a conversation.

- I know that I have immediate tools to hand which work for me in problem solving.

- I can also choose my friends on a clearer basis.

This practical use of values is not just an exercise. It is a working tool which will improve almost anything. If I know what my values are then I can see where I am doing well and where I need improvement.

Also, when a person or company considers what their values are and how these values operate then that person or company will be less likely to bully, and less likely to tolerate bullying when they see it.

There are times also when timidity isn't the issue, but being outnumbered is — and this is when workplace mobbing takes place. This is when one person sets a ball rolling, and as happens regularly on social media, a gang or mob forms and targets one individual. In many instances of bullying behaviour, bullying individuals will attempt to start mobs, by the use of gossip and by isolating their target as the 'other'. When this works it is the most painful type of bullying imaginable, and very hard for anyone to come back from.

One expert on this behaviour is Janice Gilligan White of The Empowered Employee. I asked Janice what she believed were the underlying conditions required for mobbing to happen.

> "Bullying is allowed and even encouraged in organisations that have toxic cultures and poor leadership, in companies that are facing an economic downturn, these places are heavily bureaucratised and are limited in advancement opportunities. But mobbing can take place anywhere a group of people coexist. All it takes is a conflict, a little bit of power, and secret, behind door conversations concerning someone's credibility. Most often mobbing begins with an unresolved conflict which the target may not even be aware of. If the conflict involves someone with power — whether actual power, as in a leadership position, or those with connections to those in leadership — the more likely mobbing will spread and the more successful it will be. Rumours and innuendos about one's credibility will begin to surface and false accusations will begin to make their way up the chain. As the target begins to defend themselves, possibly exposing a secret agenda or posing a risk of litigation, permission is then often

granted to deal with the 'troublemaker'. Many targets of mobbing are outspoken individuals with high ethical values and good reputations. They often feel a false sense of security that the truth, proof of no wrong doing, and their prior reputation and proven dedication to the company will save them from the wrongful accusations and character attacks they will face, but instead, they find the groundwork of those looking to take them down has taken hold. The more the target speaks out and defends themselves, the stronger the attacks become, the more others will distance themselves, and the more retaliation they will face — until they are either fired, or they leave on their own to save their health."

Sounds like a trap? It is. Although targets of bullying at work always wish they had been more prepared, it seems that when bullying behaviour escalates to mob behaviour, there really is no way out. It's for that reason that those who care about dealing with bullying behaviour and preventing it in the first place, exercise their minds in trying to establish what if any, the warning signs may be.

Janice Gilligan White:

"There are many warning signs that are commonplace. Toxic leaders are a warning sign that your workplace is unsafe and that mobbing might occur. My bullying-to-mobbing story began with a new toxic leader who micromanaged, blamed others, was untruthful and took credit for others' work. The fact that this was allowed within the organisation was a warning sign. My next red flag was that false accusations began to pop up over the course of a couple of months. The false accusations escalated in severity. What started as a false accusation of incorrectly following a policy, to racism, to an investigation into theft — I found myself busy defending myself without follow-up or fair closure on the issues. Other warnings concerning bogus accusations, are the lack of information they supply about the charges; conducting investigations that are allowed to linger without follow-up; and the lack of answers to questions asked. Following this was a surprise Performance Improvement Plan. This appeared without any prior documentation of poor performance and threatened my employment. I then continued to face criticism of my work and character, was supported less in my job, had my ability to take decisions removed, and my general ability to do my job successfully was damaged. Finally, I was moved to a different work area, and I failed my yearly review — the first bad review of my life. As this was taking place, co-workers also began to distance themselves and some turned their backs. When I did talk to few co-workers that I still felt safe with, I would have to do so behind closed doors or away from public view, increasing the isolation of my peers. Looking back, the biggest advice I would give myself would have been to leave sooner — to recognise that things were not

> turning around. Normally, if there is a conflict in a healthy environment, it can be handled quickly and effectively. As a target of workplace mobbing, you find yourself in a situation that is not improving, and which is in fact, escalating. A situation where you feel increasingly isolated, and one in which your health is affected. These are your biggest indicators that you are being mobbed."

A final value that applies to targets of workplace mistreatment is authority. The type of authority I am referring to is the authority targets have over their own story and anybody's ability to challenge it.

When the target of workplace bullying feels like they have no friends and no support, they can still maintain an authority over what happened to them. Authority is something that bullies may try and take away, but targets must resist this and must be able to say to themselves, and with honesty: "I was bullied and it was not acceptable."

Having considered what your values are, you may next find that living up to them can be hard work. We have to work at these values, sometimes, and as with all work, there are rewards and a sense of achievement.

If you have an anti-bullying policy at work that is gathering virtual dust on a computer drive, it is the same as espousing values that you do not live up to.

This is dishonest and it can be the downfall of a productive workgroup. We have all seen people who have bullied their way into positions of power.

One of the reasons these people are able to do so is because values are ignored.

In a good workplace we not only list our values, but we check several times a year that they are actually implemented and not just professed. And this is something that we can and should do together.

In the meantime — let's meet the workplace bully. Brace yourselves!

BULLY

Also known as: The One Who Exhibits Bullying Behaviour. Other than that, there is no other word for you. You're a bully and that's it. Sometimes we refer to you as the abuser. But a bully is what you are.

THE ANGRIEST PERSON IN THE ROOM

Watching our colleagues interact can be fascinating. What I admire is that while we are all so different, we voluntarily collect under these umbrellas of activity called work, and get things done.

At work our personalities are largely evident to others, while at the same time, certain aspects of ourselves are also helpfully put to one side. A wise manager is aware of the different personality types and can at least acknowledge them and support them — if not achieve more. Most of us learn to moderate our impulses and get on with other people, and working with that in mind, we find ways of expressing what we want. The rules of accommodation require that we make allowances for each other, and that is something that perhaps applies more to working life than it does to other aspects of our experience. We cannot for example, choose our families quite so readily.

There is no such thing as a bully-personality-type, and bullies at work don't so much spring into being, but rather, they usually evolve from circumstances. There are people who have bullied their way through life and left former and forgotten targets behind them. Serial bullies are not entirely uncommon and may for example be the type of people who think that the best method of getting their way is an angry fit. Yet, there is still not a typical 'bully' — there are merely bullying behaviours.

Bullying is a pattern more than it is an individual action or circumstance. It's a relationship, but it is an uneven one. Bullying is also a set of questions and challenges for a target, but they are always the wrong questions. A target wants to know for example why nothing they can say or do is correct. Deep down, a target wants to know why they have become such a problem to another person. The pain the target feels is because there are no answers to these questions. What has happened is that a bullying individual has made that target person the issue.

This is why when you are the target of a bully, nothing you can say or do will be good enough. When you are the target of a bully, the issue has ceased to be the contentions of the workplace and has become you as a person. This is one of the plainest justifications we most commonly find for bullying behaviour.

In bullying situations, these justifying sets of circumstances are presented as valid reasons for bad behaviours. This is in turn why people who know they are carrying out bullying behaviours, are still not aware that they are 'bullies'.

When the issue becomes another person, then there can only be one resolution for a bully — that other person has to go. Since bullies are working on this consciously or even subconsciously, they are always at an advantage when it comes to their target, who presumably is trying to get on with their job. It also explains why bullies at work seek the cover of bystanders, whom they will try to get onside.

Here we find the logic behind one of the most important lines a bully will use, the killer: "and everyone else agrees." If you have heard this said, then you are likely already in the bully-zone. People should speak for themselves and so when a bully criticises or insults another person and adds that everyone else agrees with them — you can remember that most well-known of bully-based songs, the infamous verse known as *Nobody Likes Me (Think I'll Go And Eat Worms)* — the ultimate musical model of loneliness and shame. This playground song iterates what every bully says to their targets: not only are you a problem to me, but everyone else thinks so too, including you now I hope.

There is a common justification for bullying behaviour concealed in plain view here. Because of their focus on a target, and the genuine belief that this target is the real issue, bullies don't see their behaviour as bullying. In light of this belief that another person is 'the problem' or simply 'someone they can't work with', their bullying behaviours are justified in their own minds. It's easy for others to see, but not for them.

If you've been bullied at work you may be able to see the facts in retrospect, laid out like the pieces of a puzzle that you are, long after the fact, only just completing. Still — you may be curious to see if what you have experienced can be classified as bullying, and this is a most valid question.

One of the best ways to approach the question as to what is — and what is not — bullying behaviour, is to find out what the issue is. If the issue is YOU, then this is a big clue.

There have been so many angry incidents in so many of our workplaces over the years, and when it comes to angry people their scenes are memorable. Anger is a part of life but what matters is how it is dealt with. It is the same as conflict in that respect — a question of management. A question even, of creativity.

Work-related anger might arise from some of the following common enough scenarios:

• Employee was promised something — a raise, promotion or an important project that did not happen;
• Employee was told to do something she felt was wrong, against company policy or incorrect;
• Employee was unable to meet a supervisor's expectations;
• Another employee is doing the same job but being paid more for it;
• Supervisor criticised employee;
• Employee feels better qualified and more skilled than their supervisor.

I'm looking at that short list of incidents that may foster anger, and I have immediately spotted a bully in there and I'd like to tell you more about them. Because if I take two of these scenarios:

• Employee was unable to meet a supervisor's expectations;

And

• Supervisor criticised an employee;

And change them as follows:

• Employee was unable to meet a supervisor's expectations, because the expectations were too high or regularly changing;

And

• Supervisor criticised an employee frequently;

— then any resulting anger becomes something more damaging and a possible instance of targeting.

That aside, the above scenarios have one thing in common insofar as they present reasonable grounds. I have not suggested how anybody could or should react to these situations — in fact all I have described are the situations themselves. All of these sketches involve employee / supervisor relationships and for me they are suggestive of conflict and not bullying — that is until I added the words 'because the expectations were too high or regularly changing' to the first one, and the word 'frequently' to the second one.

Out of control anger is one of the worst things that people can regularly experience at work, and it creates fear. There are people in our workplaces who know that others are afraid of them, and they do nothing about it. Fear is something bullying individuals use. Fear serves them and helps them get their way. "So what if you find me scary? That's your problem." We all know people who quietly appreciate their reputations, if they are known to be either intimidating or aggressive. But we often fail to look at it from their point of view and ask why they might wish to preserve those reputations, and why they are insistent that these issues are other people's problems, anyway?

All the same — verbal and physical anger with colleagues is not acceptable in the workplace, and I'd ask you to make a note to yourself the next time you see it — or the next time you do it yourself.

Anger like this might be a sign of a potential or actual bully and can be predicated on such things as:

Dislike — the bully may not like their target for any number of reasons, such as for example the target's efficiency, or popularity. For this reason, it is common for people to start a relationship as friends, but for that relationship to degrade into bullying when it becomes competitive. There are as many reasons to dislike people as there are people — but a display of anger is not the correct response to those who do not meet our private criteria for what makes a good person.

Disappointment — when goals are not met, scapegoating may commence. It is common to begin a working relationship assuming the best of someone, but when things go wrong, some people move directly to anger, instead of choosing something more appropriate, like constructive repair. In the absence of such constructive improvement, a bully will commence a campaign expressing their disappointment. This is hard for targets because the behavioural fault is with the bully's response, although the target's work will be made the issue. A display of anger is not the correct response, however, to those who do not meet our private criteria for what makes a good worker.

Worry — when work becomes stressful, responses can be unpredictable. There may be a frustrating situation or problem at work, but anger will never be a healthy response. Yet there are those that have learned from parents, spouses and others that anger can be used to motivate. This is why bullies allow their anger to become a part of their work, and once they get away with it once, they get away with it all the time. Anger however, is not the correct response to frustration at work.

While an angry person may be frustrated with you for a valid reason, they will be wrong to lose their temper with you at work. Shouting fits and abusive language aren't always bullying, but an angry outburst can be apologised for, reconciled and everyone can move on. A further consideration is that when a bullying individual is angry, a certain incompetence in their own work is also signalled.

This is the actual incompetence of bullying individuals revealed: instead of handling a situation some people will automatically make a target person the issue. This makes a bullying individual feel better, because they feel like they have dealt with an issue by dealing with the person they have targeted.

When a bully chooses to use anger at work, we are

seeing incompetence writ large. And incompetence always costs, whether avoidable or not. If your recourse to a challenging situation at work is to yell at someone else, you have already revealed an unfortunately high level of incompetence. When you double-down on that behaviour and refuse to make amends or acknowledge your anger, you might as well get the BULLY tattoo on your fists and be done with it. You are a big bully — and even if people might not say it to your face, they will be thinking it.

Some people who experience this type of anger and cannot manage it, end up living on the reputation! The trick is that those around them only see the anger and they don't see the incompetence — and that is probably the way the angry person would like it. All that it takes for others to see through this is this knowledge that anger equals incompetence. Instead of seeing anger, they should see incompetence. The two are the same.

Because bullying situations often develop over periods of time, patterns and excuses become embedded in workgroups. But if you want to know who to beware of in any group, whether it is a family or a working environment — I would ask you to check out that visibly angry man or woman — the one who is always angry with someone else. Being angry does not make you a bully. I can't emphasise that enough. Anger is normal and angry people who don't know how to deal with their feelings can privately be very unhappy. Bullying individuals really believe that certain other people are in and of themselves problematic. Meanwhile, anger is transferable like any emotion. In real terms, if a bully is unhappy, they will make their targets unhappy too. The same applies to anger.

What would you say? Does someone 'lose it' in a meeting once a year? Does it happen every month — or more than that? What is the correct response when someone for example, calls names or carries out any number of transgressive behaviours which may frighten others? Does everybody in the room know that shouting and other displays of anger are not acceptable? And are we ready to get used to calling this type of anger what it really is — emotional abuse?

WHO'S A BULLY?

We would like to present some characteristics of bullying behaviour and show how these characteristics help identify who is a bullying individual — even if it is you.

These characteristics do not vary from place to place and from bully to bully and if they don't exist in a situation, what you are looking at may not be bullying.

Like racism, bullying is something that people accuse other people of doing. There are very few people who, when they are demonstrated to have acted in a racist manner, hold up their hands up and say: "Yes I am a racist."

In the same way, a bully will never set out to be a bully and will of course talk down bullying, if required to do so. The private thoughts of racists and bullies will include racist and bullying ideas that they may not even recognise as such. A racist may admit that they have distinct problems with certain people, but these problems will be couched as presentable 'truths'. Racist people like to argue that even though they are not racist, certain statistics bear out their opinions and so that what they are delivering are not racist ideas, but facts. The commonality here is justification, and this is why bullying can be a slippery thing to prove. This is also the reason why accusations of bullying are so serious, because we are talking about the last thing anybody wants to be and the one thing that no one will ever own up to.

Bullying individuals throw everything in the path of this. This might even include the "you calling me a bully is a form of bullying" accusation. This argument is not uncommon and bullies do defend themselves by accusing their target in this way. Generally, this is a backward and anxious recourse. When this accusation is made, a bullying individual is scraping the old bully barrel and finding very little to work with. There are correct and obvious ways to respond to the accusation of bullying, and an angry scene that includes calling another person 'the real bully', is not a legitimate one.

It is a reminder however that the entire burden for an accusation of bullying falls upon the target.

They, the bullying individual, can stand with their arms folded for years, staring their target down as they stare everyone else down, denying what their target is saying. They are the acknowledged world expert in their target's faults and will never tire of listing them, especially if it will save their face. One of the lessons of meeting the workplace bully is that these men and women are unlikely to change, kind of similar to the family bully, the marital bully, and also similar to the racist.

Hence that arms-folded stance. Making an accusation of bullying has never to my knowledge 'un-bullied' someone who has embarked upon a campaign of bullying at work. The B word in fact tends to make bullies double-down — and that is why it's key that we are all able to differentiate between aspects of our working lives such as our performance, and examples of mistreatment which are much clearer cut.

It's the same with a racist. Calling someone a racist enforces within that person the ideas that led you to call them that, and so it consolidates the hostility. Calling someone a racist often makes things worse because it starts a discussion which every racist is prepared for. Such discussions can make those who began them look weak, because they may be accused of straightforward name-calling.

I've been taught that the best way to deal with any situation is to try kindness. Courtesy, thoughtfulness and fellow feeling can hardly fail as moral choices, but as practical solutions they do ship with some challenges. Whether you are the target of workplace abuse, or the target of accusations of it, it follows that while not everyone is to be believed, everyone is to be listened to and their stories heard in a safe and respectful way.

If it is true that we can all potentially resort to bullying behaviours, it should follow that every accusation of workplace mistreatment requires an arbiter. If a company cannot make an arbiter available then you automatically have a dysfunctional company. I've heard several arguments over the course of writing as to why certain companies have not been able to provide an arbiter of some kind when it came to staff complaints of mistreatment, and these have included:

- "The company is too small or there are no resources"
- "The complainant is not to be believed" and
- "There isn't time for this kind of procedure"

Here is where good managers begin to navigate like masters. In fact I'd consider the successful handling of an accusation of bullying, harassment or mistreatment to be among the greatest achievements of good managers.

I have worked in places where complaints of bullying have been ignored, sometimes consistently so. Sometimes these complaints have not even been passed on to anybody else. Failure to act on a report of bullying is a sign of unfit management — plus it is also itself bullying behaviour to ignore such complaints.

These are the worst instances of BULLY, INC. and these are the places where bullying behaviours have taken hold. Complaints about bullying are often ignored because they are considered to be small, but that is sometimes to be expected because bullying is not a single action, and can go on for a long time — even years. Specifically, targets must prepare a portmanteau argument which will shine a light on one focal point — the bullying behaviour. To themselves bullies have justifications aplenty and they can even walk away from these conversations saying:

"I'm not a bully, but …"

Every manager should be equipped and ready to deal with these issues. This will increase their chances of being a good manager. Ted Coiné:

> "Excellence in any endeavour is rare — which is how you define excellence, after all: better than the rest of the field. Unfortunately, for a lot of employees that means that excellent leadership is rare — and that's what a healthy company culture requires: excellent leadership. A leader has to understand the virtuous

> circle that brings profits. That circle begins with hiring talented, customer-centric people. It continues by doing what it takes to keep those talented employees and managers happy in their work, and happy with their company. Only highly engaged, talented people seek creative ways to problem solve for customers and to innovate at the level required in today's highly fluid, always morphing business environment. To be painfully honest, few leaders are beyond the lip service stage of caring about the engagement and happiness of their workers. I'd also warn that it's easier to find a better leader than it is to get a mediocre leader to suddenly turn into someone special."

Bullying behaviour is always the same, but will depend on the organisation in which it occurs. The circumstances and effects of bullying behaviours are always different, and perhaps this is what clouds these matters for us. It is also why in every case in which bullying behaviour is not identified, the behaviour will amplify — continue — and eventually become the norm. The situations are always different, but the beahviours remain the same.

In starting a new job there isn't any way to tell if it is going to be a success. When we start out in our new job, we make no provision whatsoever for failure. In fact, failure will be the last thing on our mind. One of the first things that happens to us in a new job is that knowingly and unknowingly we assess some fundamentals concerning our new colleagues. It is still appropriate at this stage to be aware of any people who may have the potential to bully. They probably won't be yelling at you at this point but there are still plenty ways to spot them — they have a regularly appearing set of singular traits. When these traits combine with problems or stresses, or irregularities in power and attitudes — then bullying begins.

The traits we are about to list are not enough in themselves. What is sufficient is that people are made to feel like they are the problem. This is a truth that is so simple it is overlooked. We know for certain that there are workplaces which have bullying going on all the time, but for a variety of reasons workers and sometimes even targets do not observe it. One such failure is expressed by Dr Debra Stewart who points out that such behaviours can often go unobserved "because bullies exude a magnificence while riding on the skills and competencies and talents of co-workers to save the day." (*Finding the Good in the Workplace Bully*, 2017).

In the meantime, although a bully will make another person the issue, here are five personality aspects that may apply to a bully at work and may be signs that this person is prone to bullying behaviour:

> ENTITLEMENT: I find it hard to place my finger on this sense of entitlement I'm talking about, and it might even be the wrong word. Sure — 'entitlement' stands for a certain kind of person that is unhappy when other people achieve success. There is that — but there is a more troubled sense of entitlement in some people, who believe that those who've achieved success got it by somehow cheating their way there — possibly through inherent advantages, nepotism or similar means. So here is what to do. When you get to work be aware of the person who bitches (for

example) about the person that did your job before you. You want to hear about the good qualities of those previous employees. You want to hear all the great things about these other people — not how they messed things up and how anyone (or everyone) had to put up with all their mistakes and other nonsense. This is a cracking, huge, glowing, raging warning sign. It doesn't need to specifically be the person that did your job before you — an entitled person like this could be talking about anyone. It could be their previous business partner or someone in another job in another firm, or it could be a friend or just a story they have heard. However, I have learned to perk up my ears when someone who is not present is being discussed in negative terms. I perk up my ears and I keep my mouth shut. The question here does not concern who believes the stories about these other people, but who understands the underlying principal. When you hear that story concerning all the people that have filled your role before you, be careful if they are grim stories of deceit and failure. That will soon be you — and if you think that you are going to be the one to buck this trend, you had better be sure you can handle it. Bullies have sharp claws but they are not just for scratching — they are also for holding on. You will probably not personally know the people that had your job before you, but you must listen carefully to what is said about them. Similarly, if you are going into a business partnership then consider what happened to the previous business partners of the person you are planning to work with. Every story that you will hear from a time-served bully, regarding all these previous people, will end in disaster and with someone else being the problem.

SHORT ON EMPATHY: Everyone needs resilience and some workplaces require that we have a heap. Most of us do have a heap of resilience, but let's not be forced to use it when reference to some key values will do a better job. Someone who has a tendency towards bullying behaviour will slip up on this truth and try and set a new standard by presenting that a low level of caring is acceptable. Do you know that meme that says 'Zero F***s Given'? I sometimes wonder why people are so proud of this. The fact is that for some people, it really is a way of life. You can picture their smug and defiant face already. "I don't give a f****!" All well and good, but it is the fact that you are so proud of it that bugs me. That's a small example but if there is a manager or a colleague planning to bulldoze you and you want to spot them before they start up the engine, this is the sort of thing to look out for. When people suffer, we suffer with them. The bulldozer is however oblivious to the pain it causes, and bullying behaviour can be justified by this low standard of caring. A low standard of care will allow a manager to yell at you and then tell everyone else a sob story about it. This is also the sort of person who always has a feud going on. If they can't get a feud with another employee, or a client or a contractor, then they'll find a fight on Facebook, or elsewhere online. Look out for this. It's what I call the 'professional fighter', and many bulldozers are professionals insofar as they can have several fights running at once. If they can't get a fight at work then they will have one with their neighbour, or anyone else, because one way or another they are always fighting. These bullies usually make themselves easier to identify by boasting to you about their fights, on and offline. The thing that allows people like this to have these fights is their lack of empathy — look it up! I had a colleague who surprised us one morning, on the first day back at work in the New Year, with the story of an altercation with the driver of a public bus. The story ended with this person telling the bus driver to "f*** off". When they told us the story at work, they were so proud of it and it seemed certain there had been an exciting hot-blooded rush involved. Not only was this person willing to talk like this to a bus driver, they could do so without taking into account the damage they might have caused. And then they came to work and boasted about it! That story about the verbal offence given to the bus driver might be a minor incident to the bully, but I bet that it wasn't to the bus driver. It happens all the time and not just to bus drivers. But there are folk out there for whom other people are simply just obstacles. Look out for them. They are commonly bullies.

NOT LEARNING FROM MISTAKES: Blame culture isn't uncommon — and it plays a large part in workplace bullying. The word 'culture' is appropriate, because if one manager is blaming people and getting away with it, you can be sure that everyone they are managing will be doing it too. If you work in one of these places where staff, clients, providers and any amount of others are blamed for everything that goes wrong, then you may well be working in a place which tacitly condones much more harmful behaviour. Some people in our workplaces really have convinced themselves that the problems we experience as workers and staff are never anything to do with us, or even themselves, and they continually blame something externalor someone else for anything that goes wrong, with it becoming less believable each time.

DRAMA: There is a strange flavour of drama to all of this and on rare occasions, the drama can be distracting or interesting to bystanders. However, most people become tired of workplace drama and ignore it. Someone at work who may be prone to bullying behaviour may well be one of these dramatics though. This is a further regularly appearing trait — look for the person about whom there is always some drama. What do I mean by the word 'drama'? I mean that there is always something happening, some theatricals or a scene to deal with. During the first weeks I spent in one job, I noticed a person that spent an inordinate amount of time walking back and fore talking to people. This was usually in some form of business capacity, and while a conversation might have started as work-related, such chats would go on for twenty minutes in each case, and always ended with the chatty-chatty person rolling their eyes at the rest of us, as if to say that the person they'd been speaking to for so long was a terrible windbag. In this workplace, most of us carried out our work in some static location, such as at a desk or at a counter — but this person was always on the move. What we noticed, was that this person wasn't really working at all. The illusion of work was however fascinating because there was always a pretext for these long chats. The reason this kind of thing can lead to bullying, is because when it starts to become apparent to someone that they're not in fact doing any work or are failing to meet their goals, they may start to look at ways of compensating — and that might be through targeting. Related behaviours to watch out for from these play-actors are angry fits, which also result from a practised deflection of work and responsibility. This points to something highly sympathetic in such a person, and it is a lack of confidence — but this is fundamentally not anyone's problem but their own. You will usually find that people who radiate this drama at work will also have a lot of it going on at home — with their neighbours, with bus drivers, on social media, with assistants in shops — anybody in fact. It's drama — and it is an authentically bad sign. What most people do when they see this sort of thing is look up from their work, watch for a bit, and then go back to what they were doing. They do this because they are taking responsibility for their work and deciding not to get involved. It can be a hard decision not to get involved — don't get me wrong —

and when the drama spills too near, you may sometimes feel that it's time to participate. If you do answer this call, however, you may be sucked in to the vortex and end up at best, wasting time. At worst, you will be bullied. Why does he insist on a twenty-minute call when a twenty second email will suffice? Why does he want to tell you about the feud with his neighbour? — and what is the point of his social media disputes anyway? It's drama, and it is another shield, usually concealing incompetence or a lack of confidence.

A CERTAIN PRIDE: Sometimes we meet people who appear to be proud of their scams and equally proud of how they have shoved their way to some kind of success or achievement, often discarding others in the process. That is to say — some of our colleagues, if you listen to them, will brag about how harshly they have in the past dealt with others. So long as listeners can run with these delusions that the person in question deserved the treatment they got, many people actually pay attention to this stuff. There isn't anything wrong with a story of someone who has got in our way and been dealt with. But this is different. At the same time, while we all sometimes treat people badly it is those who are proud of it that may be bullies. Some of you will already know that this pride is a further huge warning sign that an oppressor is in the room. Some will fail to see these signs, however, and follow along. Others will see these signs, and incorrectly assume that they won't be the next to suffer. That's why 'pride' is on this list, despite its being a nuanced quantity. It's all right for people to have their own way of doing things. But people who are so convinced of their methods that they look down on those who disagree with them are more likely to be prone to use bullying behaviours — often because they have had successes in the past. Some people in management and other positions of power are where they are because of what they have achieved. But when self-belief takes over, and individuals act on the opinion that what they are doing is absolutely right — then pride can lead a person (blindly) into bullying behaviour. While past successes show our experience, we need to demonstrate to every single person that we work with that we know what we are doing. When we start believing that people should act in a certain way simply because of 'who we are' or 'what we have already achieved' — then we may have already started on the path to workplace bullying.

*

None of these characteristics point by themselves to a certain case of workplace bullying. Instead they are behavioural signs which sit out with the norms of what we know to be healthy working practice. They are also behaviours which can be kept in check by company values.

Nobody is out to change the personality of the individual who is bullying another person, but instead we should be trying to maintain their behaviours within the scope of our values.

Bullying can then be viewed as a collection of behaviours, which represent values that we do not all share. Once we have identified these behaviours and the values which support them, we can determine how many of these are at play and to what extent.

Therapist Gabriella Clarke agrees that while there is not a definitive answer to who is more likely to be a bullying individual, we can still highlight trends and repeated areas of interest.

> "Some bullies are sociopaths who have self-awareness but are unable to understand empathy, so their self-awareness brings no benefit to the workplace. Most bullies lack emotional intelligence although training them in this will only be of any benefit if they value the feelings and wellbeing of those around them. On a deeper level some bullies are deeply unhappy with themselves. They don't feel in control of their lives, so they try to exert control over others. They often struggle with anger and frustration, and project these emotions onto those around them."

Most of us can never know if this is true or not. We can't look into the minds of the people who bully, any more than we can see into their past or witness the problems in their home lives.

However their workplace behaviours are often observable. There are without doubt traits which can lead certain individuals to find bullying behaviour more attractive and, in their eyes, effective. These traits listed above might not be agreeable to us all, but we can still work with people who exhibit them.

While bullying behaviour cannot be undone, the word 'bully' is different because it is a label. If you feel it applies to you then get to work in peeling that label off.

It can be done.

THE OFFICIAL DEFINITION

In their advice for employees, ACAS, the Advisory, Conciliation and Arbitration Service in Great Britain give the following definitions of harassment. It is taken from The Harassment Act:

> "Harassment, in general terms, is unwanted conduct affecting the dignity of men and women in the workplace. The key is that the actions or comments are viewed as demeaning and unacceptable to the recipient."

The advice goes on:

> "Bullying may be characterised as offensive, intimidating, malicious or insulting behaviour, an abuse or misuse of power through means intended to undermine, humiliate, denigrate or injure the recipient."

The legal definition of harassment is clear. It requires the behaviour to have 'the purpose or effect of violating people's dignity or creating an intimidating, hostile, degrading, humiliating or offensive environment.'

As far as this legal definition goes, there is an awful lot to prove in there. A target may well read that defintion and recognise the bully in their life, sitting there quite comfortably, and able to justify their actions. But this is what a bullying individual will do, because in their mind they belong in the workplace and their target does not. A bully will argue that you need to be tough in business — or that there is a personality clash, or that someone "just doesn't fit into the team" — there can be any number of excuses which they feel are appropriate. What a bullying person will be trying to achieve with these kind of statements is a lowering of the general standard of care while at the same time minimising the other — as exampled in a statement such as: "you're too sensitive."

The reason the bully can do this is because of the burdens of proof that are required in that legal definition. The above definition takes about two seconds to read and yet people spend months and even years trying to prove that any of these things actually happened to them. During which time, their health will worsen, and their bully will remain at large, able in many cases to continue bothering them and others.

I emphasise this definition and its problems for the following reason: while the correct thing to do if you are bullied is to seek official recourse via tribunal or another method, can you cope with the long wait for closure? Can your health and finances sustain the campaign?

This is not an either / or situation and I will suggest other routes which will guide you to a much earlier closure and to a formal acknowledgement of what your bully has deliberately done to you. If this acknowledgement extends to a tribunal or even a legal case, ACAS and other public bodies and charities will guide you through this process.

A useful book about bullying and the law, which includes full details concerning tribunals and other types of legal hearings, is *Fighting Back: Overcoming Bullying in the Workplace* (2002), by David Graves. This book discusses the many legal demands, settlements and statutes that you will have to be familiar with if you are going to law concerning workplace mistreatment.

Whether or not a target makes an official complaint, or begins by talking to a manager, if you are the target of workplace bullying, you are required to show a particular type of strength which derives only from your personal zero-tolerance approach to the subject.

This is what I call your authority over your story. Holding on to this authority is no mean feat. It's a bit like being on an aeroplane and being told to take the 'brace' position and finding that several months on, you are still holding that same position. This tension is a natural response to bullying and it can be depleting.

I still find the above definition of bullying to be helpful however and ACAS in the United Kingdom are at the time of publication piloting a programme which they will offer to workplaces in order to prevent harassment of this sort, and help people deal with it by explaining the fundamental legal grounds which operate in these situations.

The official definition of bullying is worth considering for what it does and does not offer. It is a confusing reminder that legal definitions can only carry us so far.

Any definition of bullying should include the following factors:

- That the activity is deliberate on the part of the bullying individual;

And

- That the activity is sustained on the part of the bullying individual.

The above definition from The Harassment Act certainly hints at these details but is not emphatic enough about intent, likely because intent is such a hard thing to prove. Breaking this down, there is a frightful conundrum in this definition of bullying, which is this — defining and illustrating the terms 'purpose' and 'effect' will take a long time if your bully wants it to.

This is because 'purpose' is hard to prove, unless you have a document or an email which states something like: "I BULLY, do willingly wish to create a degrading, humiliating or offensive environment" — which is unlikely.

And as for effect — that is easy to show. A workplace may be shown to be a degrading, humiliating or offensive environment, and yet who am I to argue that the bully has made it this way? And even if the bully has made it this way, then what if the bully argues that somebody else's behaviour is the problem, and that they are only trying to make things better?

Definitions are handy and not just for those making decisions about what and what is not bullying. But at times these official definitions may seem to lack a much-needed clarity. If this document had said, for example, that bullying could be defined as:

- Shouting in someone's face that their work is rubbish

— then yes, we can safely say that the person who did that was a proven bully. It is even simpler than that. If this document had said that getting people to do what you want by using anger or the threat of anger was bullying, then yes, we can safely say that the person who did that was a proven bully.

It is the same for everyone who has left a job due to mistreatment. No definition can properly cover the extent, the duration and emotional abuse contained in such an episode. I mention this because we are going to have to talk about proof at some point. Mistreatment can be difficult for targets to discuss and many targets have to put up with a lot before they even think about making an accusation. A target will come to their definition of bullying through asking themselves if what they were experiencing was bullying or not — and for this reason the word 'mistreatment' can be useful.

The idea here is to be careful in analysing what is happening if you feel you are a target of bullying, or if you are seeing it around you. There may be a temptation to succumb to what is known as 'confirmation bias' — assuming that you are being bullied and then using the Internet to prove that to yourself. Something can be easy to demonstrate in your own mind with your own judge and jury at work, but it may not look so convincing to others when aired.

Instead do as the lamas recommend and empty your mind — then approach these documents as objectively as you can, almost as if you were researching them for someone else.

This is why BULLY, INC, is so hung up on behaviours, because it is the actions of others than must be described and accounted for. Bullying is a world of secrecy. There is so much behaviour that goes on in private, or behind closed doors, as well as behaviour that seems to be one thing on the surface, but which has a sinister aim. It can take months for one person to remove another by means of bullying behaviour, and secrecy is the reason.

The number of people who get away with bullying behaviours at work is for these reasons alone, very high indeed. The success rate of workplace bullies is so high, not just because of the problems of finding and presenting proof, but because of secrecy. In the majority of cases that BULLY, INC. has come across, the bully has got away with their behaviour because nobody has known about it — not even the target on some occasions. When a target has left a workplace however, and even when people are certain that it has been because of bullying, there may still be no records, no witnesses, and no one to tell the story. And that's the way the bullying individuals like it.

BULLIES BEHAVING BADLY

Whether someone is a bully or not depends on that person's actions and behaviour. If you want to establish if a person is a bully, consider their behaviour. He or she has the right to a fair hearing.

If 'bully' is a description of a person, then what lies downstream of that are labels. Labels are different from descriptions in that they are theories, or hypotheses if you like.

We sometimes argue that labels are not helpful but that's only when people are uncomfortable with them. Labels are useful, otherwise we wouldn't use them. It's for this reason that we'd ask everyone not to be afraid to look at labels, and ask which if any of them apply.

There are plenty labels levelled at bullies — they are narcissistic and are psychopaths and sociopaths, we sometimes hear — and we sometimes even hear this from people who don't know the differences between what these labels mean.

It is unlikely that these labels will however be that useful, and generally we acknowledge this by simply using them and walking away. That's the key. The label doesn't mean anything if you just stick it on and expect it to hold. Labels allow us to make sense of a situation or a person, but they are not definitive, and they are not in any way 'true'. Instead labels are a shorthand way of describing things. That's why 'bully' is a label and 'bullying behaviour' is not.

Labels usually exemplify an extreme form of thinking and they tend to make the labelled person somewhat invisible, because they reduce them to just one thing.

If for example you were to say, "my project didn't come together the way I wanted it to," you may be accurately describing a situation. If you looked at the same situation and said: "I am a failure regarding that project," you'd be applying an unhelpful label to yourself.

This is the power of labels. See how this works. You have given yourself a hard time over something — and it didn't need to happen that way — and now you are marked as a failure and as such you will be less likely to succeed in future. Of course, if you label yourself as a failure, you will always reduce your chances of success.

This difference is important even if it seems extreme. The US government website stopbullying.gov, does not call anyone a 'bully', and refers to them instead as 'the person who bullied.' Such a distinction challenges the very premise of there being such a person as a 'workplace bully' — although most of the time and for the purposes of discussion, I am usually comfortable in labelling people who carry out bullying behaviour as 'bullies'!

There is a time and a place for labels however and it is still best not to label a person as a bully at work and in front of others, and at the same time wise to talk about behaviours rather than personalities. This is because the label will fail to carry with it the facts.

There are three general issues which apply to all such labelling, whether we are dealing with adults or children who bully. Firstly, labels send a message that a person's behaviour doesn't change from one situation to the next. It is possible that someone may bully another person at work, and yet watch in anxiety as a friend in another place of work is bullied. They may even be bullied themselves elsewhere, such as online.

Secondly, labels suggest that behaviour is well-established and not likely to improve. Much as we may find that 'bully's gonna bully', behaviour can of course change for the better. A person who has been shown to have bullied a colleague may be given a second chance, and yet this won't work if the label 'bully' has been stuck to them and is associated with them over the longer term.

Thirdly, labels can be harmful, because they send a message that tells a person how to think about themselves. A message such as "you are a bully" may carry an implication like: "You have an enduring property and I am judging it," as opposed to: "You have bullied someone and it is time for you to apologise and improve."

It may well be true that a person who is seen to bully once is, in fact bullying their way through life and will bully again and again — in fact I think it's common. That said, a label is still unlikely to be helpful to that person. In her book *Mindset: The New Psychology of Success*, Stanford University psychologist Carol Dweck argues: "When you're given a positive label, you're afraid of losing it, and when you're hit with a negative label, you're afraid of deserving it."

You can see how the labels 'victim' and 'bully' will fail in light of this. I feel in this instance that when people label themselves as 'victims,' they may without knowing it be sending a message that they are weak or deserving of sympathy, when what they may actually need is emotional help dealing with a dreadful situation.

The reason the definition of bullying does not change across the board is because beyond the label, the same behaviours appear to manifest, and across all workplaces. One of the best surveys of these behaviours is from the Workplace Bullying Institute (workplacebullying.org) and it is a list titled *'Top 25 Workplace Bullying Tactics'*. This was compiled by Dr Gary Namie, and is a reminder of the sort of things that definitely should not be happening at work — or anywhere else for that matter.

The percentage figures indicate the amount of bullied individuals who reported these behaviours:

1. Being falsely accused of errors that were not actually made. (71%)
2. Staring and glaring — nonverbally intimidating looks which clearly show hostility. (68%)
3. Discounting of a target's thoughts or feelings with comments such as "oh, that's silly" or similar low-level emotional abuse. (64%)
4. Use of the 'silent treatment' to either stall or end communication, and sometimes used to separate a target from others. (64%)
5. A bully exhibits what onlookers must presume are uncontrollable mood swings in front of others. (61%)
6. A bully made up their own rules on the fly that even

they did not follow. (61%)
7. Disregarding of satisfactory or exemplary quality of work despite evidence — including withholding of praise. (58%)
8. A bully harshly and constantly criticised a target because they have set a different standard for them. (57%)
9. A bullying individual started or failed to stop destructive rumours or gossip about another person. (56%)
10. A bully encouraged bystanders to turn against a targeted person. (55%)
11. A bully singled out and isolated one person from co-workers, either socially or physically. (54%)
12. The bully publicly displayed unpleasant, undignified, but not illegal, behaviour. (53%)
13. Bully yelled or threw tantrums in private or in front of others to humiliate a target; in short, has failed to communicate peacefully. (53%)
14. Stealing credit for work done by others. (47%)
15. A bully abused the evaluation process by lying about the target individual's performance. (46%)
16. A bully called their target insubordinate or criticised them for failing to follow arbitrary commands. (46%)
17. A bully used confidential information about a target individual to humiliate them, either privately or publicly. (45%)
18. A bullying individual retaliated against a target after a complaint was filed. (45%)
19. A bully made verbal put-downs or insults based on gender, race, accent, language, or disability. (44%)
20. A bully assigned a target undesirable work as

punishment for something. (44%)
21. A bully issued unachievable demands involving for example, workload, deadlines and duties for a person being singled out. (44%)
22. Launching a baseless campaign to remove a targeted individual. (Often this is not stopped by the employer) (43%)
23. A bully encouraged a target individual to quit or transfer rather than to face more mistreatment. (43%)
24. A bully sabotaged a targeted person's contribution to a team goal or reward. (41%)
25. A bully ensured failure of person's project by not performing required tasks, such as signoffs, taking calls, and working with collaborators. (40%)

These are some of the most common possible actions occurring in an instance of workplace bullying. For someone who has been labelled a bully, they may be surprising. This is because someone who has carried out any of these actions against another may not have quite added up the emotional, financial and career damage that these behaviours can cause. Indeed, a bully might just see one or two of these and think that they constitute deserved and justified actions at an appropriate time. These actions and combinations of them are going on all the time, and all around us at work. These behaviours go on in politics and the media, and we can witness them being played out there. What is missing however is an aware voice indicating that these are in fact bullying behaviours.

People who are bullied out of their jobs never get

over their experience. Workplace bullying really is a spiky ball which can never be handled without it hurting. If you have carried out any of the above behaviours and someone has left their job as a result, either by being forced out or because they have simply run away — then you should think about this life sentence you have handed on. When you speak to people who have been bullied out of a job, you will always find the same thing. People who are bullied out of their jobs rarely get over their experience.

Such knowledge may help a target of bullying when they get to their next job if they are at a stage in their life at which they are able to find another job. This is because what hurts in adult bullying is the knowledge that you as a target have every right to be in the job you are in, and that this has been taken away — usually by a combination of some of the above listed behaviours.

Those who bully know that most of the actions on the list can't be legislated against and that they can rely on bystanders to look the other way. Virtually everything on the above list can in fact be carried out in secret, which is why people leave jobs, and why bullies succeed. If bystanders won't become involved, then the only things stopping a bully are their empathy (which you could call their consciences), their impulse control and their competence. Bullies have to look in the mirror too, and even with the above list in mind, they still have to do so while saying: "I am not a bully."

This brings us back to labels. Labels can be applied as easily as they can be peeled off, and this is their utility. Labels are different from behaviours, which can be judged by anyone to have taken place or not, regardless of justification — and we should all be aware of them.

This is why The Workplace Bullying Institute's list has been reprinted here. It's because when it comes to look in the mirror, we can all ask: "Am I bully?"

The following story, from an anonymous interviewee, demonstrates that our actions can be bullying, and have an effect, without our really knowing it:

> "I used to work in an IT department. It was very blokey. We were the lads and always mucking about. To this day I still feel bad about the way we treated one guy who quite obviously didn't want to be part of our gang. Because of that he quickly became the butt of jokes — none of which were intended to be vicious, but they probably were. He was very decent about it and seemed to take everything in his stride. Then one day he just disappeared. Didn't even bother to resign. A few weeks later I saw him in a pub and went up to him to see how he was doing. He told me to 'f*** off'. I honestly didn't get why he was so angry, so I asked him. He told me how I and my mates had made work miserable for him and how he had dreaded going in every day. I'd completely read him wrong and hadn't realised the truth: we had all bullied him."

WOMEN BULLYING MEN / MEN BULLYING WOMEN

Some issues regarding bullying behaviours are straightforward and others require us to find honest answers within ourselves. The recovery from a bullying experience for someone who has been a target will involve a whole lot of soul-searching.

The reason it's a whole lot of soul-searching is because your answers need to be honest and correct.

Being forced out of a job is something a person never forgets. That is because such situations are unfair and may not have been resolved, and maybe they never will be. There will also be questions which may never properly leave a target's mind.

To ensure the final answers are both honest and correct, this takes a lot of time. The experience of being bullied is entirely negative but targets will know when they've started to emerge from it because they'll begin to formulate some answers.

Perhaps protected characteristics will come into play at some point, and these are generally written into an anti-bullying policy like this:

This policy covers unlawful and harmful behaviour that involves harassment or other unwanted behaviour related to:

1. Age
2. Being or becoming a transsexual person
3. Being married or being in a civil partnership
4. Being pregnant or on maternity leave
5. Capability
6. Nationality, ethnic or national origin
7. Religion and belief or lack of religion and belief
8. Sex
9. Sexual orientation

These are the nine protected characteristics that are defined in the UK Equality Act of 2010, which states that individuals and groups should not be discriminated against on any of these bases. In the United States these are known as 'protected groups', and although they are federally mandated they vary slightly from state to state and include an individual's military veteran status and their genetic information — as defined in the Genetic Information Non-discrimination Act of 2008.

The scope of such policies is always widening, and for some people they are only widening to become narrower. We have talked to a woman who left her job after a case of acknowledged bullying in which management attempted to shoehorn the details of the bullying behaviour into a narrative concerning ethnicity and gender. The story is worth telling here because even though the person that was bullied was a woman of a certain nationality, no suggestion was ever made by either herself or witnesses that this was behind the bullying. These characteristics however surfaced in the management's final report concerning the mistreatment. The target in this instance did state that she felt this was a personal matter, and not one of gender and ethnicity. She also stated in resigning that this suggestion somewhat devalued her experience, which she believed was personal and not related to any of the listed characteristics.

These characteristics, which are synonymous with the nine safeguarded characteristics that are written into UK law, became 'protected' in order to clarify situations under the Equality Act in 2014 — meaning that it is illegal to discriminate against people on the grounds of these. This invites us to have a closer look at the concept of discrimination, which is fundamentally a tool which we use to make decisions.

When an employer takes on a new employee, they may do so by discriminating between people who are good for the job (for example due to experience) and those who are not. The Act correctly enforces the idea that these decisions cannot be made on any of the above grounds. Experience is therefore a valid ground for discrimination, while age is not.

These same grounds have found their way into laws and regulations concerning dignity at work and are especially useful in these areas in that they define quite specific abuses. These protected characteristics exist because it has been shown that people of these categories continue to be discriminated against in many different ways — and although this is useful, bullies are indiscriminate.

Time and again, bullies go for people that have something they want. Often this is a position of power, no matter how trivial it might seem to others. We spoke to somebody that was targeted because her bully wanted to be the one that ran the company Facebook account — a matter that nobody else cared about. At a higher level company directors and business partners may be found bullying each other in order to gain company control, but at all levels, a bullying individual will usually have a goal in mind. In obsessing about their target however, bullies give themselves away.

Bullies in general therefore have a firm idea of who and who does not fit in to their working environment. And it happens sometimes that those who don't fit in to the bully's worldview, don't fit because they do not share these same characteristics — e.g. a woman in a team of men, or a Muslim in a predominately unreligious group. In these situations, the protected characteristic becomes the tool the bully uses, as opposed to the end. In the cases of discrimination that the Equality Acts of both the United States and the United Kingdom were set up to counter, the discrimination is usually the end in itself.

There are several ways to devise anti-bullying policies, and one of the best is to have the staff compose the policies themselves, making reference to these legal definitions where need be. An anti-bullying policy is an essential for every workplace, and is put in place to protect both the staff and the organisation. Even in cases where a company owner may be bullying others, there is a still a legal entity which is the company, and this must be said to exist as separate. On top of this, the right not to be bullied persists whether there is a policy in place or not.

Grey areas regarding what is and what is not bullying,

and statements concerning protected rights, are however often next to useless. People require support and guidance at work, and it is the job of a manger to provide it, not policies. If support and guidance are not a part of any managerial process at your place of work, the door is wide open for bullying.

Sometimes, the terminology used concerns me. The part of most workplace policy documents which deal with bullying usually say something along the lines that there is a 'no-tolerance approach to bullying of individuals based on race, gender, religion, and sexuality.'

This is the sort of thing we give the nod to, and yet while it is possible for racism and sexism to be a part of bullying, the two things are usually separate. That is not to say that racist bullying does not take place — it really does. It is true that racism can be a part of bullying and that racism can be a reason for bullying — and racist violence, harassment and abuse are so closely related to bullying that it is difficult to distinguish them. Racist bullying at work can range from poorly-considered remarks which are not necessarily intended to be hurtful, to deliberate physical attacks. Key however, is that as with other aspects of bullying, racist bullying can be identified by the motivation of the bully. As in all cases of workplace bullying a range of behaviours needs to be considered, as does the language used. In cases of racist bullying, targets may be singled out because of — among other things — the colour of their skin, the way they talk, their ethnic grouping or by religious or cultural practices.

The same thing applies to sex and gender. BULLY, INC. has come across relatively few women who have told us that they were bullied *because they were a woman.* The same applies to men. In groups, exclusions can arise however, and people may be picked upon for being different. Statistics do not work here because the criteria of bullying are generally tangential to these factors.

In the case of men and women, there are a varied set of statistics regarding propensities. Statistics do exist reporting who is most likely to bully who, and while they are interesting, they are generally of little use and less comfort. Some articles state quite plainly that men are more likely to bully women — and nobody could in honesty have a problem with that possibility, even if it is not borne out by their own experience. What we may have a problem with is the fact that when a person does bully another person, they should not feel that they are afforded a certain cover by a statistic.

In our opinion there is potential here for confusion. For example, the introduction of gender can in some circumstances make bullying into something it is not. Bullies generally do not bully because they are prejudiced, but a bully will use any tool they can, and if gender seems an appropriate way for them to dominate or hurt another, then so be it. A bullying individual may well target a person based on what they imagine are the characteristics of that person or even that person's gender, but the gender will not usually be the end point.

Gabriella Clarke, who has experience of dealing with the targets of bullying says that in her experience yes, the male to female ratio is about even. This highlights a difference between bullying and sexual harassment. While sexual harassment occurs overwhelmingly to women and is carried out by men, bullying is far less likely to be based on any characteristic in its targets.

Any of us can be found to be at a disadvantage in this respect — but bullying does not happen because of any bully-provoking characteristics in ourselves. It goes on because of the lack of integrity of bullies.

A particular concern is mental health. People are made unwell by bullying to begin with — and I note that mental health — while it could be said to lie under 'capability' — is not a characteristic that is automatically 'protected'.

Protected characteristics in the workplace are still useful however and cases which involve these protected characteristics tend to be treated more seriously, and that is probably wise. Certainly, cases which involve protected characteristics are probably going to be easier to define and witness — but we always return to the same fact: it's not excusable to bully people on any grounds, and key to the issue of bullying is the objective nature of what has occurred, not who it has occurred between.

In the instance of bullying by gender, there remain inconsistencies. Taking the two groups MEN and WOMEN and trying to attach propensities to each is possible, but ultimately it fails. It is sometimes said, for example, that someone is much more likely to be bullied if they lack self-confidence, and even if that were true, I have seen no evidence to suggest that one sex is more likely to lack confidence than the other.

Further, bullying statistics by gender, race and religion also demonstrate that different situations produce different outcomes. While it may be argued that broadly speaking, persons of one gender or ethnicity are more likely to be bullied, these statistics don't come anywhere near meeting the actual criteria of real bullying cases. That's because in real bullying cases, people of low self-confidence, and people with mental health complications sometimes suffer these issues *because* of the bullying. Certainly, workplace bullying will worsen these symptoms.

If this needs to be shown in any concrete way, let us quickly discuss the gender pay gap.

While (nearly) everyone agrees the gender pay gap is a real thing, which can be demonstrated by any number of statistics, nobody is suggesting that this is down to bullying. This is because we instinctively understand bullying to be about something else. Across the board there exists a specific unfairness to women, and a part of this is down to the fact that some men in positions of power have a tendency to want to choose men over women. Also it turns out that some men are prejudiced. Some male employers are even open about the fact that they don't like employing women because they don't want to pay maternity leave, and in saying that they are openly ignoring the Equality Act. What this displays is not bullying however, but prejudice.

Whether by a man or by a woman, and directed at either a man or a woman, bullying remains separate from bigotry. Bullies may be bigots and bigots may be bullies, but trying to equate the two can be counterproductive.

What we recommend is that you check your own company's anti-bullying policy. It may well need updating. In the ideal workplace, you and your colleagues would check this anti-bullying policy together and do so in light of your company's stated values. At the meeting, which should be held at least yearly, everyone should be made aware of the values of the company and the behaviours that are expected, as well as the impact which more negative behaviours can have.

It is essential that when anti-bullying policies are put in place that they are discussed with everyone in the company or workgroup, and that discussion of what bullying is remains out in the open. We can even write our own anti-bullying policies. This is in fact the preferred method at BULLY, INC. because it allows everyone the opportunity to carry out that most important of conversations — the conversation about bullying.

That way, workers will seek more healthy ways of dealing with conflict, grievance and disagreement. Discussion of bullying with references to such values and policies shines a light on it — and as bullying is a dark art, that light will cause these abusive behaviours to wither and hopefully never take root again.

BULLY #METOO

Sexual harassment, according to Professor of History at The New School in NYC, Claire Potter, "uses the erotic to conceal what it really is: bullying." (The Guardian, 10.02.2018).

The #MeToo movement is an ongoing public action which spread virally in October 2017 in order to demonstrate the widespread prevalence of sexual assault and harassment — especially in the workplace.

The movement took off after multiple sexual misconduct allegations were made against Hollywood mogul Harvey Weinstein, and in discussing this case, Claire Potter goes on:

> "Noteworthy in his own world for widespread cruelty and violence, [Harvey Weinstein] was a screamer, and used his size, influence and explosive rages to intimidate both men and women …. He also bullied people with money, using his immense wealth to create a web of legal restraints designed to silence critics and potential truth-tellers inside and outside his company."

The phrase 'Me Too' was first used in 2006 by social activist Tarana Burke but became globally popular in October 2017, in light of the Weinstein stories. To this day tens, if not hundreds of thousands of #MeToo stories, virtually all of them from women, exist on YouTube, blogs and other Internet platforms. Perhaps, as with other workplace bullying stories, the epidemic didn't just concern the abuse itself but the discussion of it — and #MeToo certainly has something to say about bullying. Even these few observations of Weinstein, above, illustrate:

- Temper tantrums and the creation of a fearful environment;
- Power abused to create restrictive or punishing circumstances for staff;
- The abuse of money as a coercive tool.

These are descriptions of what a bully at work might act like. That bully might be a sex pest, but more likely they are an angry manager or an autocratic small business owner. Hence we are interested to know where #MeToo and bullying meet, as there is clearly more than just an overlap. Individual instances of sexual assault or harassment may be separated from more commonly witnessed campaigns of bullying — but in the case of harassment, there are usually going to be longer term patterns.

One #MeToo story that has a general resonance is that of Christine Blasey Ford. Ford is a professor of psychology at Palo Alto University, who in September 2018, publicly alleged that then-U.S. Supreme Court nominee Brett

Kavanaugh sexually assaulted her when they were teenagers in the summer of 1982. She testified about her allegations during a Senate Judiciary Committee hearing regarding Kavanaugh's Supreme Court nomination later that month, and as a result her case became something of a simultaneous byword for both being believed — and not being believed.

Christine Blasey Ford's story is relevant because it demonstrates something which commonly occurs in all bullying stories. To consider this, we'd ask you to imagine that somebody did something hurtful to you. Then imagine that person denied what happened or perhaps they remained non-committal or acted like they did not care. Then imagine that when you told other people about what happened, they either doubted what you said or found another way to remove your authority. Then imagine that in light of this, your authority was further muddied by counter-accusations against you — and other stories which presented yourself as the problem.

This is familiar territory. Targets of bullying may not be aware of what is coming when they make accusations of workplace abuse, but often this is when things get worse for them.

Anything can and will be used against a target of bullying and not just by a bully. Targets who speak out should be prepared for their mental state to be challenged, as well as their own motives and activities. Targets should also be aware that they may be ignored, and that this may be extremely painful.

What the #MeToo movement highlighted first was a long-standing problem concerning the propensities of certain men in the workplace. Secondarily however, and even if it did not mean to do so, the #MeToo stories indicated how a preponderance of evidence can be effective in reaching conclusions.

For example: long before he was convicted of rape and sexual assault, there was a consensus in the eyes of the world that Harvey Weinstein was a sexual predator of the worst kind — and yet none of us were witness to any of the abuses that we had heard about and that were alleged. I would suggest this consensus emerged because a large amount of credible accusations created a preponderance of evidence which we accepted to be true. The reason that so many people accepted the accusations against Harvey Weinstein to be truthful, was because the stories told by his targets were consistent and credible, and the target individuals were able to talk to the public and were largely supported by the media and each other in doing so.

This is when bullies begin to be outed, but not always in a healthy way. If I ask you, who is more likely to be a bully — a person with several accusations of bullying made against them — or a person with no accusations of bullying made against them — then what would you say?

Preponderance of evidence, then, even if it points to a kind of pitchfork justice, is still used by people, whether they know it or not. So, we may find ourselves coming to conclusions based on nothing more than hearsay when we hear anecdotally about individuals whom in some cases, we don't even know.

As bullying is sometimes such a hard thing to prove and as most workplace bullying cases do not go to a court of any kind, then a similar preponderance of evidence is sometimes played out.

Sexual harassment cases vary immensely in scope and seriousness. Sometimes they can be resolved because they involve a well-intentioned person saying the wrong thing to the wrong person. If such situations are dealt with kindly then restitution should be possible, because it is certainly true that some people don't know the right words to use in order not to trigger or upset others. 'Kindly' here means mediated discussion — it does not mean posting about the incident on social media and hoping for a mob reaction, because painting people as harassers and bullies will never end well. This is because it looks like we are discussing personal flaws in others and not their behaviour.

The truth or falsity of a target's allegations can at times, therefore, sadly became irrelevant. People who didn't want Christine Blasey Ford's accusation to be true attacked her credibility — what in technical terms we couild refer to as her authority over her story. As Christine Blasey Ford's story was globally broadcast, we as bystanders were constantly invited not to consider the bullying behaviour we were hearing about, but instead pointed towards the personal flaws in both the target and the accused.

Each instance of harassment will be different, but it remains the case that where sexual abuse and harassment occur, the workplace culture is usually a bad one and other wrongdoings are condoned. Repeated instances of flirtation or over-familiar expression, for example, will absolutely constitute bullying because of the degrading long-term effect they will have on a target. This is indeed where 'the erotic' — as described by Claire Potter — moves to conceal bullying. It is simply a matter of the bullying person using the available tools.

Reading about this unpleasant culture in the entertainment industry, most of us remain on the outside looking in. Closer to home, it's harder to be brave and outspoken about our own workplaces. One thing we have learned from the entertainment industry and #MeToo is that open secrets are not uncommon and that such open secrets can allow abuses to persist for extended periods of time, even decades. Here, company boards and managers who claim ignorance either don't know what's going on or they are lying — and neither are acceptable.

This suggests that complicity is just as big an issue as bullying itself. Another thing we have learned from #MeToo that applies to all workplace bullying, is that to save their skins, bullies have to implicate their targets, turning them into villains. In understanding these kind of activities and how these situations play out, #MeToo shows us that when a serious allegation is made, the accused will do everything they can to discredit the accuser. They will fight back — and discrediting their targets is one of their safest bets.

Bullies, as we shall see later, no matter what the environment, have only one place to hide — and that is in the opinions of bystanders.

THE STING OF THE QUEEN BEE: ALL IN THE MIND?

Queen Bee Syndrome. Sounds nasty doesn't it? Inflicting pain. Demanding attention. Implying a central player and an audience of drones. This term has been used to label instances when women bully other women, or more specifically where one – the Queen – bullies.

An equivalent term for men bullying other men a work? No, we've not come across one.

The idea that there is even such a thing as Queen Bee Syndrome might suggest a significant set of capabilities in women — almost like a sub-branch of bullying. When men bully men, it's not called anything, but when women bully women, we need bigger science. Maybe the phrase 'alpha female' has something uncomfortable in it, as if we just don't like the sound of it. Labels are not helpful, and in matters of bullying, the more labels we use, the worse we may make things. Labels can be self-fulfilling too. Does a woman identified as a 'bully' inevitably have to live with being identified as a 'Queen Bee' as well?

'Queen Bee' is a putdown as well as a label. It is an uncomfortable descriptor for a female that treats others in a condescending and most likely aggressive manner — probably regardless of gender. It's someone who expects others to assume what she wants or needs, and it's really language more suited to the Urban Dictionary than the workplace. Its existence in the vernacular suggests that women are being judged hard.

The statistics that cover women bullying women need to be dug into a little. And if you thought science needed a special term for women bullying women, you'd be wrong.

The Workplace Bullying Institute's 2017 survey reported the following bullying stats:

M -> F — 65%
M -> M — 35%
F -> F — 67%
F -> M — 33%

The survey shows that women are more likely to be the targets of bullying — and that is all. According to this research, men and women appear to bully to the same degree and have the same statistical tendencies. And they tend to bully women.

So why do we have Queen Bee Syndrome, a term used to describe woman on woman bullying, and not a syndrome to describe what is actually the reality — the fact that women are more likely to be bullied than men? Some might argue we do have a name for that syndrome — 'The Patriarchy'.

The idea of the Queen Bee at work first arose in the 1980s when Dutch psychologist Naomi Ellemers was trying to figure out the near-total absence of senior women in academia. Women, she discovered, made up just 4% of all professors in Holland, and Ellemers wanted to find out if discriminatory men were keeping women from advancing.

When she had mailed every female and many of the male professors in the country with her survey, Ellemers found that women, also, were a part of the problem. The female professors she interviewed not only felt unsupported by their female colleagues, but they didn't want to work with other women either.

Over a decade later, when Ellemers surveyed doctoral students and university faculty members in Holland and Italy, she found similar results among senior women, who displayed negative tendencies towards their female colleagues. And she called these women 'queen bees', because they coped with gender discrimination by accentuating how different they were from other women.

The distinction which Ellemers highlighted proved too subtle for the world at large however, and she was disheartened to read news articles which used her research to argue that women were somehow vindictive by nature. In fact, the entire syndrome is now considered an actual tool of that above mentioned 'Patriarchy'.

'Queen Bee syndrome' among women at work was identified as a myth by researchers at Columbia Business School in New York, who claimed that a lack of women in top roles was due to men's determination to retain control. 'Queen Bee syndrome' — displayed by leading professional women who keep other females out — was a myth, according to the study.

This new research looked at top management teams in

1,500 companies over a 20-year period and found that where women had been appointed as chief executive, other women were more likely to make it into senior positions.

But when a woman had been given a senior role that was not the top position, the likelihood of other women following them to executive level fell by 50%. (The Guardian, 07.06.2015)

The truth of Professor Ellemers' research is therefore something more understated. But it would go something like this: successful women emphasise the ways they're not like other women and also downplay the prevalence of sexism.

We could add to that: women are judged to a higher standard than men, and not just by men.

At the same time, most people feel that there are behaviours that are more likely to be used by women. Bullying prevention advocate and author Sherri Gordon writes on verywellmind.com and in her books that there are specific behaviours favoured by these 'office mean girls', as she calls them. What she shows are a set of behaviours that in her view appear to be concretely attached to women and girls. She argues that women tend more than men to use exclusion; they struggle with envy; they often steal work or take credit where it's not due; they lie, gossip and spread rumours. Most surprisingly of all, Sherri Gordon seems to argue that women are more likely to be serial bullies, who struggle with anger; and finally that they are power hungry.

In 2012, Kim Elsesser, from the Center for Study of Women at UCLA carried out a massive survey on people's perceptions about women at work and found:

"The study of 60,470 women and men examined

> evaluations of participants' current managers as well as their preferences for male and female managers, in general. Across-sex bias emerged in the ratings of one's current boss, where men judged their female bosses more favourably and women judged male bosses more favourably. The quality of relationships between subordinates and managers were the same for competent male and female managers."

In 2016 Elsesser expanded on this work and published her *Handbook On The Well-being Of Working Women*, writing:

> "Substantial empirical evidence supports the existence of bias against female leaders. However, a closer examination reveals that much greater bias is exhibited in studies where hypothetical or laboratory-created leaders are studied, and little or no bias is exhibited against women who actually hold leadership positions."

The unholy corollary of this data is that whatever it is we think about women — it is in the mind. Kim Elsesser's research suggests that in the day to day practise of our lives we are much more likely to treat people equally than we are in the abstract.

Critically, if we are allowed to make decisions about people based on our perceptions of them, it appears we are much more negative, especially about women. When it comes to real life and interactions, our behaviour is fairer it appears. The abstract is our world of perceptions, based on fears, assumptions and opinions, and the real experience is more balanced. Perhaps this is why life online is particularly dangerous for women, because everything is more anchored in the abstract and thereby less real.

How you think about the world as well as your prejudices and preformed opinions make a big difference here. Those who believe that women are feelers and men are thinkers, are inclined to wonder for example, if women are more likely to consider that they're being harassed or demeaned, compared to men under equivalent circumstances.

The answers are in how we perceive the world. When ditchthelabel.org carried out its ground-breaking research on how people perceive masculinity and femininity through social media discourse they discovered among other things that:

- One in three of all discussions associated with masculinity on Twitter referred to violence; and that
- Crying was the second most mentioned subject associated with masculinity

These are fascinating results because they indicate that we all hold the keys in our minds, concerning how we think of each other. Analysing three million misogynistic tweets, the same survey found that 52% of those three million tweets, were written by women.

If Queen Bee Syndrome is something that we need to pay special attention to, we also need to explain some women's disparagement of other women. In academic circles this is known as 'system justification,' a psychological concept whereby groups which identify as being to a degree oppressed internalise negative stereotypes as they struggle to make sense of an unfair and discriminatory world.

Queen Bee Syndrome boils down to this: the subject seeks a validation that hinges on denigrating her peers. You could also call it 'managing while female'. The reality is that a lot of people, whether they are aware of it or not, struggle to deal with a strong women in a professional context, maybe even more so when that woman is in charge.

This is a classic Catch-22 situation: women can't break into important jobs unless they advocate for themselves and command respect. Thus, if you believe in it, Queen Bee Syndrome almost becomes a professional inevitability, not just for women seeking to climb the corporate ladder, but for any woman interested in a long and winning career.

OUR DEFINITION

Labelling a person as a bully is not a good idea — but sometimes it turns out that there is no other word. If you have carried out bullying behaviour and remain unrepentant about it — you are a bully.

In the words of Mary O'Neill:

> "Bullies don't admit to bullying — they don't show up in counselling — and they don't volunteer for research studies!"

The word 'bully' is a label, and it is a label that everybody is scared of. People may get upset and call each other 'bully' when mud-flinging situations arise, but we must be on the lookout for certain behaviours and not rush to judgement when we hear the word 'bully' being used about someone. Some targets survive for months in their workplace, suffering the malign behaviour of another person and doing so without recourse to the B-word. This will be because the person carrying out the bullying is not unacceptable to them. It will be them, the target, that is unacceptable to the bully. There often comes a time however when the word 'bully' becomes unavoidable, and this threshold is crossed when the bullying spills from less obvious behaviours into more confrontational actions that others can observe.

There is a tension here, reflected in all cases of workplace bullying. Because bullying behaviour is allowed to take root and become normalised, an awful lot of bullying may have gone on before a workplace is able to collectively identify it. When it comes to challenging the behaviour and calling out the bully, it is sometimes too late. Somebody may have already lost their job and people's health may be compromised.

It may be true that in order for someone to correctly assert that they have been bullied they need to have been bullied for quite a long time, and consistently so. It is a painful fact of life but with bullies in the workplace, we sometimes come to know them by their results. These results often need to be manifest to be known — and are things like ill health, people leaving suddenly, unexplained absences, upset individuals and so on

It is this same lack of knowledge regarding the makeup of the 'typical bully', which according to expert Mary O'Neill, sometimes causes them to be referred to in research literature as 'black holes'. Much of what we know about people who bully is learned from their targets. There can be no bullies without there having been bullying behaviours — and there can be no bullying behaviours without people becoming ill or otherwise rendered less capable than is to be expected. Trying to identify bullies before they have hurt anyone is going to be fraught with issues, and so we generally know who the bullies are by the colleagues they have hurt.

This is why prevention in the form of shared values works so well. When behaviours are observed, we can ask if these behaviours are in line with company values or not, and we can act when they are not.

Such behaviours should only constitute bullying if they take place:

Repeatedly — There's no set number of times that bullying conduct needs to occur, although in most instances, it must occur more than once;
Unreasonably — The test here is objective and is assessed from the point of view of a 'reasonable person, having regard to the circumstances'. This is semi-legal language for a variety of norms, such as common sense and decency. It is a universal definition, which looks at what a hypothetical reasonable person might have done in similar circumstances. As an example, sitting down with me to discuss an issue might be considered reasonable — yelling at me in anger would not; and
As a Risk to Health and Safety — This implies that only a possibility of danger needs to be shown, not an actual danger to health and safety. Bullying behaviour in the workplace is usually identifiable in terms of the well-being of those targeted and for this reason bullying must be considered a health issue.

Definitions of bullying don't vary much from place to place. The only places the definitions of bullying are unclear, in fact, are in the minds of bullies — and this is a problem. The psychology of the bully is hard to pin down and unlike their behaviour, does vary widely. I asked therapist Mary O'Neill, however, if she believed that the bullying instinct is one learned in childhood and taken into adult life — and she gave me a simple answer: yes.

> "I believe what we learn in childhood is taken into adult life," she said. "Our coping strategies as children are more likely to be the ones we resort to as adults under pressure. It's what we know — it worked for us then (or so we imagine) and so we think: why not give it a go again? The trouble is that as adults those strategies are redundant because we're more mature and we know better. That said, we still resort to old behaviours."

In light of her experience in Transactional Analysis, I was interested to hear Mary's thoughts about this Adult / Child relationship in patterns exhibited by bullies.

> "Bullying is not an Adult process," said Mary. "When people bully, they are resorting to behavioural strategies that they think worked in the past. So, for example: I didn't get my way as a Child, so I threw a tantrum and mum and dad relented. Now when I want people to do what I say I throw a hissy fit and terrify them into obeying."

This fear which Mary describes can persist at a low level in places where workers make decisions based on what they think will cause a certain supervisor to retain their calm. If you are sort of person who moves through the workplace trailing blue touch-paper behind you, this is your issue however! It's not for you to blame those who may inadvertently light it.

Although it is of scant comfort to targets, there is always a question with bullies regarding whether they act with malicious intent or are simply somehow afflicted with behaviours which they cannot control. After all, no bully identifies as such.

> "Some people like Gary Namie who runs the Workplace Bullying Institute in the USA will state yes, bullies do act with malicious intent," says Mary. "However, Laura Crawshaw of the Boss Whispering Institute, who is one of the few researchers who works with abrasive leaders, disagrees. She states that the bullying manager who is shouting and so forth is feeling threatened and resorts to a fight or flight response — and in this case they're in fight mode. Laura Crawshaw does acknowledge that some manipulative bullies exist, and they may well have malicious intent, but they are not as common as we think — and they can even be coached to adapt their behaviour."

The fundamental behaviours associated with bullying do not change however, no matter what causes them. We should all be aware of these behaviours and talk about them in regular team meetings, so that we can assess them, rather than assessing each other. That way targets do not need to wait until they are ill before they take action, whether it is official action or evasive action. Mary O' Neill's extensive research data is in agreement with other research data. She has found that bullies at work tend to be critical and blaming, withholding and untrustworthy — and so this is something to watch out for:

> "When it comes to bullying there are those that argue that bullying is about behaviour rather than personality — and yet there seem to be common behavioural traits most often displayed by bullies. The withholding, for example, can be anything from information, praise, entitlements and rewards — and it is a little power play. People who bully therefore tend to lack empathy towards others and so are likely to criticise others without considering why they might behave like that. That's why sending bullies on leadership training programmes or even coaching programmes can be pointless as they will sit in the audience completely convinced that the message doesn't apply to them. Bullies aren't very good at reflecting on their behaviour. It's why they never come to counselling. They tend to blame others for failure and don't take responsibility for mistakes."

Laura Crawshaw manages this distinction between behaviours and personalities carefully, stating that abrasive managers are terrified of failing, but because they lack insight, reflective skills and empathy, they resort (out of fear) to spiky and critical behaviours. The use of language here is fascinating, because although people who are known to use bullying behaviours at work will never go to counselling, I believe that Laura Crashaw has a huge success rate in sending them to what is effectively counselling, just by calling it 'coaching'.

There is also a 'Snakes in Suits' definition of bullying which seeks to describe the activities of people labelled as 'psychopaths in the workplace'.

> "Yes," says Mary, "these people exist but they are not the major source of bullying in the workplace. If your manager is a psychopath — leave."

While a hurtful or seemingly unpleasant person might be abrasive, we can't just look at them and on those grounds say: "bully". Labels such as 'psychopath' or 'narcissist' may have a certain currency, but these are clinical terms and so they are not our business.

Our business is bullying behaviour and that is what we must define. For sound practical reasons we are therefore advised to think about other people's behaviour, which in cases of bullying often begins with the low-level stuff — the criticism, the withholding and the blaming — before it develops into other worse behaviours. Only then will we be on our way to where we want to be — ANTI-BULLY, INC — the company in which we are all attentive bystanders, working to the tune of some shared values which everyone can relate to.

Bystanders, after all, have the power to end bullying behaviour in any workplace, by standing up for the target or by reporting it, and by most of all knowing what constitutes bullying, preferably in relation to some shared values.

The next question to answer is why bystanders don't always intervene, and what they can expect if they do. All of us are after all bystanders, some, if not all of the time.

BYSTANDER

Also known as: witness, supporter, sympathiser, neutral party, observer, upholder of rights, onlooker, colleague, friend, personnel, the other workers, team members, staff.

ALL THIS YELLING IS HURTING MY HEAD

Our environment has an impact on us, something which extends 100% to the workplace and the people in it. Our working environment will change who we are and how we feel about ourselves, as will our home environment and the neighbourhood in which we live. Even social media platforms can change who we are — because they are environments.

In these closed spheres that I am describing as 'environments', we both act and react — and because they are closed spheres, people who may behave in a healthy manner in one context can become a target in another. Similarly, people who might be reasonable in one context can succumb to repeated bullying behaviours in another.

Think of that normally plausible personality who becomes a demon on Twitter. You can spot bullying behaviour easily on that platform, because there are so many people using it who don't respond to discussion with discussion, but with insult. Commonly, group behaviour on

Twitter is ideological, but routine mobbing can be based on anything driven by the news or similar. Twitter has proved to be such a corrosive method of discourse because it is so reductive, and with communication being limited to 280 characters, it is not a platform suited to subtle discussion or expression.

For bullying individuals this is ideal because of the temptation to make their opponent the issue. It's a failure to remain on subject and a tendency to attack a person — hallmarks of bullying behaviour and observable to others.

It is this notion of observable behaviour that we return to because when bullying becomes observable it is time for the bystanders to make decisions. When there are open or suggested abuses in the workplace and we see people suffering, it is still common for some of us to say:

"I'm just going to stay out of it"

Or:

"This is nothing to do with me"

In reality however there is no such neutrality. Once you have observed the suffering around you, you are already involved. The reason the 'none of my business' type of response is common, is because in most cases bystanders don't know what to do or are scared of the bullying person. Understandable. But the reason steering clear of trouble should not be an option is the difference between conforming to a situation or transforming it. Conforming to the suffering of others will not only change you for the worse, but allow the genetics of bullying and all its values to mutate a once healthy workplace into a place of torment, at first for the one — then for the many.

When bystanders intervene and behaviours are acknowledged, larger transformations do however ensue.

I would ask us all to give some consideration to observing the difference between:

> Someone who occasionally uses an aggressive tone, overbearing body language and / or heated words to convey anger and can acknowledge this and make amends;

And:

> Someone who is responsible for bullying behaviours.

The two are not the same. Simply yelling at someone does not make a person a bully. For sure you will have a grievance after being yelled at, but bullying is about much more than one single action. Bullying is about patterns of behaviour which are usually known to bystanders — known, and often ignored for a variety of reasons.

Acknowledging this, I know that I've witnessed shouting and fighting going on in various workplaces and over a long time, and yet I still wonder: why did it take me so long to question its acceptability?

The uncomfortable conclusion that I've had to reach is that over the years I have at times been a bystander to workplace bullying. I'm not alone, because we've all been bystanders at some time — we all know about it — but we often freeze when we see it happening.

Taking temper tantrunms and shouting as an extremely obvious example, I accept for starters that shouting at people happens. By this I mean that we may all find that there are times when a voice is raised in anger. We might be driving and yell at another motorist. Just about every parent yells at their children at some point — and when someone hurts us — even by accident — we might find ourselves shouting back in response. These moments are probably to be avoided but that doesn't mean we shouldn't ask ourselves what is going on. And I call the example of temper trantrums and shouting 'extremely obvious' because they are usually a form of bullying that other people (i.e. bystanders) are aware of.

I will share an example from my own experience, because I have fond memories of it. Indeed — fond memories of a boss who used to yell in anger — and quite a lot of the time!

When I worked in the filing department of a bank, our team leader was a former military man who sometimes shouted at the staff. Despite this I would not say he was a bully. It happened every so often that this guy would yell at one of us for something. When this happened a general scene ensued, and this team leader would raise his voice. Each scene concluded with hurt pride as targets and bystanders skulked away into the long rows of files and gossiped about the incident.

What had happened was that our team of twenty had been hired at the same time, and of this hire, this man had been chosen as our leader because he displayed an authority which the bank bosses had liked. What this former soldier promised was that with an army-like efficiency, he would somehow create a well-drilled workplace.

Well-drilled was right! This man had been in the army since he'd left school and done well there. But at the bank there was one memorable afternoon when this same leader tried to get our team to march up and down. All twenty of us — marching! He did this in the earnest belief that it would improve our team's performance, and he did it because he had no other tools to enforce discipline.

The responsibility for this situation lay with the bank's managers. This ex-army man was a poor hire as team leader. He had no team-leading skills relevant to a banking environment, and yet the managers believed that they could take work practises from the military and impose them where they were never going to work. The yelling done by this team leader, his drilling us and some of the other more comic aspects of this scenario, were attributable to our team leader's need to meet the bank's targets. As team leader he was given more money and had an extra responsibility to ensure that the job was done. However, the bank misjudged his ability to do this.

Yet — I do not believe this was workplace bullying and I do not believe that he was a workplace bully. This was because every yelling incident at that job ended the same way — the grievances would be met head on, the ex-soldier would join us in a team meeting, and sometimes also at the local pub. Notably, such fiascos always ended with apologies if they were needed and discussions about how we might try different approaches. We would talk about it and the ex-milityary team leader would express his frustration at not being able to 'control us'. Once everything was out in the open, the team leader's honesty was always appreciated. The ex-soldier was at heart a genuinely nice guy, who wanted to be a part of our team — not the controller of it. If you picture him at all, you must picture this man as wanting to be one of us — and yet he could not find a way of achieving that while simultaneously doing his job. Finally, the team leader was removed from our department and was found a more suitable role elsewhere, and here I am today, still having fond memories of that afternoon when he tried to get us to march up and down on the bank premises! I can't say I was that impressed about it at the time, but he made conscious amends.

This is not a tale of bullying. It is a tale of poor decision making, learning and even one of fellowship. We were all in it together — I still believe that.

In an instance of bullying, things are different, because often the aggression will not be acknowledged, far less apologised for. A bully will yell at somebody and expect that to be the end of the matter, sometimes because of their authority. In an instance of bullying, yelling in anger will be justified by any number of excuses, perhaps as it possibly still is in schools and homes. In both environments there is often a 'person in charge' mentality, which is certainly something that bullies like to adhere to. A bully on Twitter also displays the 'person in charge' mentality, because their belief that they are correct about whatever issue is causing the dispute, justifies their denigration of others.

I like the idea of acknowledgement because it allows for healing. Every process of emotional repair begins with acknowledgement and this is where bystanders can honestly help. Once a person has been mistreated by bullying at work, acknowledgment that what happened, actually happened, is one of the most psychologically beneficial processes there is. It can be helpful if such acknowledgement is dealt with in 'public' in the sense that it is witnessed by other staff, but that is not always appropriate.

What is important is that a company's values dictate that acknowledgement of bullying behaviour has happened, and that everybody knows this to be the case.

When it comes to raised voices at work, this is a transparent sign that there may be bullying going on. I say transparent, because outbursts of anger are hard to conceal. Often it is to the bully's advantage that they have a reputation for being 'hot-headed', let's say, because it creates an atmosphere of fear which can be motivating for all the wrong reasons. In this fashion, a bullying individual confuses the unease of others as a sign of their esteem, or their power — but the principle here is that angry people can be frightening because they are unpredictable, and nobody likes to be yelled at.

Yelling in itself may be a negotiable matter, but acknowledgment is not. If you cannot get acknowledgement in a case of bullying behaviour at work then there is never going to be a chance of restitution, and a person who has been targeted is going to remain in a limbo where that yelling is still ringing in their head.

I would advise anyone who has yelled at someone else at work to acknowledge what they have done as soon as possible. If a grievance meeting is not convened or any similar solution, then what started as someone losing their temper begins to smell a lot like bullying.

Think of it like this — every hour that passes between an angry flare-up and the acknowledgement of that behaviour, is an hour of lost productivity. If you want to bring your workplace to its knees, then the quick way to do it is to have a temper tantrum and leave it unacknowledged. A person prone to bullying will commit a verbal abuse like this and then double down, arguing that they were provoked. This behaviour is wrong, however, and delaying the point of restitution costs health, money and productivity.

The first rule of communication is that you must trust that what the other person is saying is truthful and well-meant. Neither of these apply to yelling incidents and in fact they do not apply to bullying in general.

A phrase I once heard stands out here: "For bullies, competence is competition."

If you are poor at your job to such an extent that you must leave that job, this will probably be obvious to you. If this is the case and you are told in a polite and calm manner that you are failing in your work, that does not constitute bullying — it's nowhere near it. If, however, you are repeatedly told that you are bad at your job, while not being offered advice or paths towards improvement, this is workplace bullying.

The challenge now becomes how to safely neutralise the behaviour of bullying individuals and educate ourselves into becoming creative bystanders. What does it mean to be a bystander to bullying at work, and what is 'the bystander effect'?

Graham Goulden of Cultivating Minds UK and the Scottish Violence Reduction Unit encourages bystanders to bullying behaviour not just to intervene, but to approach bullying with the view that what is needed are conversations around behaviour and social norms. In discussing this process, and how bullies may be able to benefit from the bystander effect, Graham writes:

> "Whilst in some situations there may be safety in numbers it is clear the larger the group the less likely anyone will take much needed responsibility. A barrier to taking responsibility is the concern about what others will think if you get it wrong. It is clear that the bystander effect has many negative outcomes for society. People ignore others who are in danger, they even put themselves in danger. The group can be a powerful influence on us."

It should be understood that being a bystander is not an easy thing. Yet there remains an ideal place — a working environment where there is no bullying. And we can only imagine that workplace as being composed entirely of well-informed bystanders.

The bystander effect is sometimes also called 'bystander apathy', and it is not a proven nor given response to bullying, but really just a claim. This claim fundamentally states that individuals are less likely to offer help to a person in distress when other people are present.

In fact, it is even said that the greater the number of bystanders, the less likely it is that one of them will help. (psycnet.apa.org: *Would I be helped? Cross-national CCTV footage shows that intervention is the norm in public conflicts.* 03.06.2019).

In specific cases of bullying, Goulden suspects the claim is yet more valid, arguing that most bystanders will condone the behaviour by ignoring it:

> "The default can often be to ignore — walk away and remain silent even when it is a work colleague or friend that is involved or impacted. We might not see it as our business or our role to intervene."

As well as inspiring individual leadership to prevent abuse in the first place, Goulden uses the keyword 'safety' — more important to most employees than they are aware — and a reminder that bullying behaviour is a matter of Health and Safety. This message concerns safe dialogues which are rarer than we might imagine. In fact, safety for dialogue sometimes only becomes something we are concerned about when it is too late.

For bystanders, Goulden argues, apathy or lack of involvement can be an unsafe route:

> "Do we ever consider the consequences of our inaction? What does our silence and inaction say to those involved or impacted?"

These are good questions, and they are hard to answer when as bystanders we more often than not decide to wait and see what will happen — before we decide what we should have done.

STANDING BY

The word 'bystander' is revealing. It expresses the fact that many of us literally 'stand by' while bullying behaviour is going on. Uncomfortable as it may be, there are no easy parts in this play.

When bullying is either secretive or subtle, bystanders may not know that it is going on, but when a bully's behaviour can be observed by others, bystanders have one major line of defence which runs along the lines of: "There are two sides to every story."

So many people have been found hiding behind this that I would urge everyone to give some thought before uttering this phrase. This phrase is a bully's best friend and an important bulwark, being the single biggest place a bully can hide. To locate that place accurately what we are saying here is that a bully at work can only hide in one place — within the opinions of colleagues.

The opinions of others are a bully's only cover. Even if they witness what they suspect is bullying behaviour, many people will still want to get on with their job — and because so much of the evidence for bullying exists between two people, it is consequently sometimes felt that there isn't a lot that other people can do. These others are left in an uncomfortable situation. They are bystanders.

When we as bystanders say things like "there are two sides to every story", what we are really trying to express is that, if at all possible, we would like to remain uninvolved. A lot of us will actively seek to remain uninvolved in a bullying incident for very good reasons, including our own safety. No workplace wants an ongoing trial in its midst as a targeted individual attempts to assert the facts of his or her situation. And nobody wants to get on the wrong side of a bully. If bullying is a Pandora's Box, there is sometimes it is felt, a common interest in leaving it closed.

That's one reason why bystanders often decide to wait and see what the outcome is — before they decide in retrospect what they should have done.

Recent research into bullying practices at work have come to a deeper appreciation of what it means to be a bystander in the face of bullying behaviours. Although bystanders are innocent of any direct abuses and remain so, how bystanders respond will make a difference. It is now a commonly accepted belief, for example, that bystanders can influence more than just the outcomes of bullying and that they are in fact pivotal to its elimination. Before this can happen, the main challenge for bystanders concerns their neutrality — because even if witnesses to workplace bullying aspire to a neutral stance — it turns out that this is so hard as to be virtually impossible.

This isn't just because we cannot be neutral about bullying — everybody must accept a zero-tolerance approach — but it's because bullying is like a whirlpool. If you happen to be too close to that whirlpool, you'll be sucked in — but even if you're not in the immediate vicinity of the vortex, it's going to have an effect. A whirlpool is a body of rotating water produced by the meeting of opposing currents — the bully and the target if you like. Such a general menace to stability will demand attention in any workplace and although people will begin to be aware of bullying activities first as a suspicion, if there are bullying behaviours in a workplace, the results of those behaviours will usually end up manifesting in quite tangible ways. Sometimes the bully gets what they want, and it might look like the whirlpool has abated. But this whirlpool doesn't stay calm for long. As bullying is an ongoing set of behaviours, bystanders may feel compromised when they become aware of it. They may suspect something is up or feel bad vibes in the air, but when they do see more concrete examples of mistreatment, they may then feel guilty because they hadn't said something earlier.

Bystanders may also be closer to the centre of the whirlpool than they know. Some bystanders encourage or even trigger more bullying by making unhelpful comments, laughing or by doing things that further stimulate a bully. Bullying behaviour comes with its own emotional rush for the bullying individual, and the possibility of increased popularity at the expense of a target can be a draw.

So although it's hard, we must catch ourselves if we find ourselves witnessing negative behaviour and doing nothing about it. Such behaviour isn't to be confused with so-called 'office politics' and nor is it to be treated as a kind of sideshow. Treat it as what it is — a threat to health and safety.

Website bullyonline.org goes further than most on the

subject of bystander behaviour, stating that its founder Tim Field believed that if workplace bullying arises, then all bystanders will become involved, either as bullies or targets. It is a dystopian image, and describes one of the worst incarnations of BULLY, INC.:

> "It's about survival: people either adopt bullying tactics themselves and thus survive by not becoming a target, or they stand up against bullying and refuse to join in, in which case they are at risk of being bullied, harassed, victimised and scapegoated until they have to resign, and / or their health is so severely impaired that they have a stress breakdown, take ill-health retirement or are dismissed on capability grounds, or otherwise find themselves unexpectedly selected for redundancy, or being dismissed on grounds of misconduct."

Even after witnessing bullying behaviours at work, most bystanders will passively accept those behaviours by doing nothing about them. In some teams, bystanders contribute to bullying problems by being the audience that a bully needs. On top of that, silent acceptance of a bullying situation also allows bullies to make headway. Sometimes, it is appropriate that bystanders step into a conflict situation, especially if one individual is very much out of line. But when it comes to health (and bullying is a health and safety issue!) there is more at stake than simply who is right and who is wrong.

So, in piecing this together, bystanders have their own specific roles and issues — in which they generally become aware of their responsibilities as a potential audience, and hesitant about their responsibilities as potential arbiters. The role of arbitration, and a feeling that they don't know 'which side to take' — is something that bystanders also accept, even when it is not being asked of them.

The first thing that bystanders should challenge then is their role as potential audience members. To visualise this, bystanders must never think of themselves as taking one person's side against another. It is not the bully that bystanders must decide about — but the bullying behaviour. In this capacity the role of bystander is an impersonal one. For bullying individuals and their targets the issues might be personal. However, the correct response of a bystander is based on the impersonal and the objective facts of a situation. A target of bullying will likely take the bullying behaviour personally, and so this is an opportunity for bystanders to role model an impersonal view of what is going on. After all, targets of bullying have only two options in saving their livelihoods and their health:

- They can either ask bullies to stop bullying;

Or:

- They can ask bystanders not to tolerate bullying.

There are no prizes for guessing which of these is more likely to have an effect — and yet bystanders not only risk being wrong about whether certain behaviour is bullying or not — but they may also risk becoming a target.

Helpful bystanders exist, but they do so at their peril.

What practices can bystanders therefore turn to that they can trust and will work for everybody?

The answer is values. Only through a practised knowledge of their company or team's values can bystanders both protect themselves and bring a bullying situation to an acceptable close.

This means that the smart thing a bystander can do is act. While bullying is a live issue, some bystanders can intervene by discouraging a bully or even defending a target but in the meantime, a declared set of values, known to each person, will form the only sure road map out of this territory.

American businessman Roy Disney put this well:

> "When your values are clear to you, making decisions becomes easier."

Even if bullying behaviour has created a fearful atmosphere, a set of unalterable values can guide everybody to a safe conclusion. If you are in a workplace which has not stated what these positive values are, there will be no possibility of repair, not only because there will be no tools for the repair, but because nobody will know what the repaired entity should look like.

In intervening, bystanders may well fear becoming targeted and this is a real concern, as is the possibility that intervention may make things worse. And bystanders have the same right to work without hassle as everyone else. The ferocity with which a bully can turn on a bystander who tries to help can be astounding, and so it is understandable that sometimes bystanders freeze. The thing that is never true of bystanders however is that the situation is none of their business. Like it or not, neutrality is not an achievable goal.

Constantly in life we're called upon to make decisions about right and wrong, and in processing these decisions, we use values. This is why it helps enormously to know what your values are as a company or workgroup.

It's therefore time to find out what your company's values are. And if your workplace does not have any anti-bullying policy and no stated group values, then I would advise any bystander to be the hero of the hour and institute these.

Every work group should have its own agreed values, and if your workplace does not have these, then do your best to make sure that these are discussed and put in place, so they are known to all. Everyone who accepts the values will thereafter be ready for any of many difficult situations.

Finally, those targeted by bullying must never involve bystanders and try and get them on side. Targets must resist this strong temptation. Although bystanders to bullying are critical to a healthy outcome, these same bystanders should not be influenced by targets. This is because even if bystanders accept what a target says — and they might not, especially if that target is already displaying anxiety about their situation — a bullying individual may be ahead of the game and be ready for this. Part of a bullying process always involves attempts to sway the feelings of others and if you think about it, manipulating colleagues in order to make another person look bad is just another example of bullying behaviour. Therefore, involving bystanders is a battle a target will definitely lose.

If you are that target of bullying behaviour then retain your dignity, even if you feel like you are suffering in silence. Bystanders can and will help, but they will do so by following organisational values and must never be approached about taking sides. The only side a bystander should be on in any case of workplace mistreatment is the side of the values. That way, bystanders to bullying maintain a safe and respectful distance from issues that will damage the health of the workplace. In doing so, they also ringfence their own well-being.

IDLE TALK COSTS LIVES

We have so much going on in our lives, and as well as our many differences, there are problems that we all share, as well as those problems which are specifically ours alone.

For these reasons I marvel that we all get along so well! With so many individual needs and so much pressure on us in so many different ways these days, it's to our credit that we get anything done at all.

It's a great thing that we accommodate each other like this, and we have gathered a few common tools to help us do so. One such tool involves the setting of boundaries — and often it is the boundaries which allow the most unaligned bunches of misfits to pull together and achieve.

Talking about each other is inevitable but there is a distinction between constructive discussion and gossip. If I ask a question or make a statement about someone who is not present, this may be for a good reason — but it also allows the opportunity for gossip. Gossip can allow bullying to go on in the most discrete way possible. But more than that, gossip has a chapter all of its own in BULLY, INC., because it is the very substructure of bullying. Whether it is at work or in the media, or in a community of any sort, gossip creates the footholds and reinforcements that bullying behaviour requires. Gossip, whether it is idle or active, seems to play a part in every instance of workplace bullying, and it is for that reason that we as bystanders should do our best to avoid it.

The power of rumours and gossip is considerable and a little of it goes a long way.

For example: imagine that just before you read this book you heard some negative rumours about me, my private life, or another story that portrayed me poorly. Would you have been so keen to read the book?

This is the great power of gossip: simply saying something can make it true. Accusations, whether they are true or false, stick like glue and slow everybody down. For bystanders as much as for targets, this will be one of the first signs that you are working in a damaging environment.

Effectively stated, in the case of gossip, what you are witnessing is a struggle between actual knowledge of what is going on and what people are in turn saying about each other. Responsibility for this lies with management, who sometimes have a tendency to link workers and goals in one straight unbreakable line. In the context of this straight line, there is a goal at one end and an employee at the other end, and there can sometimes be very little in-between. What this means is that some people, not trained in observing and maintaining company values, begin to see other people as obstacles. As people exchange gossip and negativity focuses on others, the slippery slope does what it does best — it slides that other person to a miserable end.

To be clear, when we say gossip, what we mean is talking

negatively about a third person who is not present. Gossip is something that takes place in every workplace, school and institution. It is observable and universal, and so we can easily look at it in behavioural terms, and use ourselves as the guinea pigs.

To do this, here is the test for gossip.

First, we establish if what we are saying is **TRUE** (as opposed to: "it was just something I heard"); then we think about whether it is **GOOD** (and it tends not to be in the case of gossip); and finally, we ask whether this information that is being exchanged is **USEFUL** — which similarly, it tends not to be.

This is known as the 'Triple Filter Test' and it is normally attributed to the ancient Greek philosopher Socrates. This test provides an ethical filter that can help us become more self-managing and respectful participants in any discussion, on and offline. It is a tool for safety.

Let us go back to that rumour you heard about me. Was that **TRUE**? I'd suggest that it's neither true nor false, and that it was a matter of opinion. Was it **GOOD**? No, it most certainly was not good, as it was intended to portray me in a poor light. And was it **USEFUL**? I would argue that it was not useful, because it makes a judgement about me which is not relevant, because what is at stake here for you as a reader is not your opinion of me, but your opinion of my book.

Despite nothing about back-biting and gossip being welcome or favourable, there is still a purpose to it. If there was not a purpose to back-biting, it would not be so common. In essence, what such back-biting does is that it elevates somebody while at the same time it seeks to disadvantage another. On top of that, such gossip makes the back-biter look more pleasing to others, because they have some interesting information. Yet it still bullying behaviour. Back-biting is bullying behaviour because it is intended to hurt. Gossip is intended to transfer power away from a target, and generally to the bullying person who is carrying out the gossip.

The gap to mind here is the distinction between perception and reality. It might also help to ask who it is that decides what you think — because sometimes you'll come to the uncomfortable conclusion that it is not yourself.

That's why when it comes to deciding whether there is bullying or not in a certain situation, back-biting and gossip are key players.

Sometimes, those who don't take part in gossip can be made to feel uncomfortable. For the same reason, when we do take part in gossip, we do so because we are trying to fit in.

We might therefore benefit from asking what sort of bystander we are. Are we the sort to nod and laugh and return to work? Are we the sort to repeat what we have heard? Or are we the sort to ignore the gossip — or even challenge it?

I'd argue here that how we respond to such gossip is going to be more important than any effort to stamp it out. I stress that if you are looking for the symptoms of bullying to either prevent it or uncover it in a workplace, I can guarantee you that gossip of one sort or another will be involved.

If as bystanders we adopt a simple model to identify these behaviours, we will be well on our way to understanding what constitutes bullying at work. Gossip is one of the observable behaviours that everyone can understand. What is known as 'water cooler chat' might have moved from the shop floor to social media groups and team management software, but the principles abide. Consequently, keeping our comments about others as civil and positive as possible, will go a long way.

Sam Farley, expert on cyber-bullying stresses this process is the same in the real world, as it is in any electronic form:

> "We still know little about the best methods of addressing bullying. However, preventative methods are superior to reactive ones and organisational level methods will likely be more effective than individual level coping strategies. With this in mind, organisational leaders have a key role to play in making it clear to employees that bullying is not acceptable, as well as role modelling how to treat employees. When bullying acts do occur, it is essential to create a climate which allows for conflict to be resolved fairly and transparently. Finally, it has been suggested that bystanders can have an important role in the coping process, by intervening against bullying and offering social support to the target."

If the climate Sam Farley describes is one of transparency, then it is important that bystanders do their best to be **true**, **good** and **useful** in talking about colleagues. While nobody can control what other people say, think or do, we can all reach clearer decisions about what is right and wrong if we look towards shared values and know that what is coming out of our own mouths at least adheres to those. If gossip complicates things at your workplace, then it may be worthwhile sharing with your manager that you'd like to see a policy to address it.

THE PUBLIC EYE

The workplace is not a public space — in fact it has more in common with a family space. If you leave home in the morning, travel through public spaces to work and then arrive at work, you have been to three types of location which are in part regulated by a set of entirely unwritten rules.

There are unwritten and unspoken rules wherever we go and those who don't accept these rules of behaviour are generally found to be either unwell or criminal — although in between these two states of being are that larger group — the antisocial.

Antisocial behaviour — which includes bullying behaviour — can be broadly and rather bluntly termed as 'bad'. That's why we say that those who are bullied, like those who are injured by criminal activity, are targeted because they are good. When we say 'good' here, we mean that these targets are accepting of and are adhering to the accepted rules. That's why when you are bullied, it is not because you are a bad person. You are bullied because you are a good person.

Although the motives of bullies vary, the consensus is

that bullies target people who present the following qualities: competence, emotional intelligence and likeability. Targets may unwittingly inflame a potential bully because they are popular, capable or have another characteristic that the bully perceives as a threat. Essentially this person is 'good' because they are following some rudimentary norms.

These norms are like pre-agreed behaviours which are generally expected of us — such as don't steal, don't hurt, and treat others with the same respect you'd like them to afford you. The good stuff. At the same time, we have many agreements with each other that we aren't even aware of, but which are still there — concerning things like acceptable levels of eye contact, for example. These are called 'normative rules' and they describe things that are required or permitted. Such normative rules tell us what we ought to do and they inform us what we should do. At work these normative rules exist to promote safety above all else, but they also foster the exact well-being that leads to productivity.

Here is a further reminder that bullying is a health and safety issue. Because if bullying behaviour goes on then safety will be at risk — and where safety fails, productivity suffers. From small businesses to nation states, where safety fails, the basics of life are often lacking, and productivity is low or non-existent. When discussing safety in a work context, we do not always mean ladders and falling items. But we also mean everyone's safety from verbal abuse, as well as other behaviours that will hurt them.

At work, whether it is stated or not, normative codes persist. We all pick up on these codes quickly and in adhering to them we feel we are a part of the organisational whole in the same way a citizen feels a part of his or her country. In a way, you are kind of a 'citizen' of your organisation, whatever it is. It could be a civil service office or it could be a family owned fishing boat — but normative ground rules persist. These codes even persist in criminal circles — especially if you think of criminality as a job! Although criminal codes are different, they oddly serve the same ends — the safety of the criminals (from the law and from each other) towards a productive (yet criminal) outcome.

Bullying behaviour is a challenge to these principles and norms, but it is not because a bully is unwell or a criminal. Bullying individuals disregard these rules because they have the will to do so. This is why they are here labelled 'antisocial'.

They key is that while we all agree there may be normative rules in a certain place, we often don't get around to discussing what these rules are. This is because rules vary from place to place, and because people are unclear as to how we define them — something a set of stated values can underpin.

A common bullying practice that bystanders will witness is the humiliation of a target. Indeed, public humiliation of a worker requires an audience. By public humiliation I am talking about an employee receiving a dressing down — or more commonly, repeated dressings down — in front of colleagues.

Cast your mind back to school. Think of the times when the class watched in fascinated fear as the teacher picked on one person and try and remember how much of your attention this took, and the shocked silence that followed. Many people suffer this at work and they do so because of bystanders freezing — a normal pack response. What we witness as bystanders in such an instance is a breach of the normative rules of our being together. We know as bystanders that if someone really does need a dressing down, the way to do it is with a quiet and kind word. We know as bystanders in a workplace, that if someone's behaviour or actions invites a reprimand, there should be management documents, somewhere, which will detail a relevant procedure.

If we reimagine such a situation and look at it in light of a common positive value such as 'respect', we can see how things might be different. Consider such a public reprimand once more, in terms of the following:

1. Respect exists as a stated organisational value. This value is discussed in staff meetings and everyone in the organisation or workgroup is aware of 'respect' as a value.

2. In light of this, bystanders are thereafter permitted to examine any activity in the workplace and challenge whether such an activity meets the provisions of this value.

3. In the case of the public humiliation of one or other workers, bystanders may objectively challenge the behaviour of the person carrying out the humiliation, by referring to the value 'respect' as the adjudicator.

Bystanders may feel that if they witness a worker being

humiliated by a manager or another person, then they could face the same sort of trouble if they speak up or act. Returning to that image from school — just imagine the difficulty a child would face in calling out such behaviour in a teacher? Anyone who calls out such things knows that they will be the next target — so why would anyone risk it?

If, however, you are responding to the value and not the person, then the arbiter is not going to be a manager or anyone else who may be drawn in to make a decision, but a higher authority — an unalterable abstract in the form of the value, here stated as 'respect'.

This is why we should focus on the normative behaviours of our workplaces and the individuals who are ignoring them. Bystanders may even come to accept such a thing as the public humiliation of one worker in particular as a kind of tolerable background noise, or as an admissible collateral damage in times of crisis. But I would impress upon all bystanders that any such bullying behaviour, including improperly delivered negative feedback can be neutralised by values. Further, such behaviour should not even happen in the first place if positive values are commonly acknowledged. If the boss in this instance had already agreed to uphold the company value of 'respect', then the question that boss must answer is this — was what they did 'respectful'?

This is how easy it is for bullies to thrive. This type of humiliation is familiar to everyone and yet it can only occur in places where there are no stated and shared values. The corollary is that bullying is common because stated and shared values are so uncommon.

Since bullies usually operate in accordance with a company's standard practices, targets can feel that they deserve the criticism they receive, and sometimes they are just too embarrassed or fearful to confront the harasser. This reluctance on behalf of the target is where bystanders armed with organisational values must help.

Every company and workgroup has values, and a tune to which it marches, and even if these values are not known, they will be there. What is important is that the values are stated, and these must be public only insofar as everybody involved knows them, and everybody agrees with them.

Values are different across all contexts and industries and it's up to us to establish what our own values are. Secrecy might be a great value for a country's intelligence services but it is hardly going to be an appropriate ethic in a sports team. Examples are numerous — but two constants remain: first is that values are there, whether we know them or not; and second is that when these values are declared, improvements in relations and productivity are guaranteed.

BYSTANDERS FEEL THE FEAR TOO

Who is more insecure — me or my bully? We could argue that one out until retirement age, but I'd be sure to give in first. That defeat would prove that the answer is always going to be — ME!

I've heard the term 'bully magnet' used by individuals who believe that one way or another they attract bullies and bullying behaviour. I can't say I like it.

Worse than this, on the subject of children bullying other children, I read statements to the effect that children who act submissively and anxiously are more likely to be bullied than children who do not. Developmental psychologist and career coach Rebecca Fraser-Thill argues (as an example) that bullied children are in her view more likely to be insecure, have less friends, be physically weak, be 'different' in some way or have overprotective parents (verywellfamily.com 08.12.2018).

What this seems to suggest is that bullied children tend to be insecure and cry often, even before the bullying begins. Similarly, other experts on the subject believe that a child's lack of assertiveness may serve as a cue to bullies that the child in question is a good target. There's evidence that children who experience depression and bodily symptoms of stress (such as headaches or stomach aches) may be more likely to be bullied. This is unfortunate since these symptoms also seem to be caused by, or worsened by bullying.

There's no obvious break in that cycle but the logic must be challenged somewhere if we are to proceed. When a cause and a symptom are the same, positive intervention is all that will fry that loop.

Often bystanders are minimally aware of bullying behaviour in workplaces, and might at most comment on a 'bad atmosphere', or something similar. Whether the indicators of bullying are observable or not, if a workplace is being run with a tinge of fear in the air then it's absolutely to the benefit of the person creating the fear that everyone be aware just how dangerous things are. There is sometimes a certain volatility around a bullying individual. Everybody knows the people who actually want others to be scared of them. Some workers may live under that uneasy shadow on an almost perpetual basis. A company value cannot and will not be scared like this.

This concerns both performance and conduct at work. Executive business coach and workplace bullying expert, Mary O'Neil:

> "In some cases, the organisation will reward aggressive behaviour. There is a difference between performance and conduct. Many people who bully may have good performance, but it is their interpersonal conduct that is poor. Organisations that fail to distinguish between the two are likely to reward the manager only on performance and ignore bad

> conduct. This is often when targets of bullying give up. They go off sick or they leave the organisation. Organisations lose millions through staff attrition, and they lose lots of experienced staff to bullying."

You may have had the opportunity as a bystander to observe somebody who has been accused of bullying. The reaction of such a person is worth noting. Generally, the way that people react when they are accused of bullying behaviour is that they will listen carefully, respond carefully and seek to restore harmony. Many people will be upset by the suggestion that they have bullied someone else but they will still want to listen and work towards repair. A bullying individual will often react to such an accusation with aggression however, and similarly may return the accusation by stating that either their accuser is a bully, or that some other person is the real bully — with aggressive denial being another common response.

This difference is marked by the fact that there is a reasonable response to the accusation of bullying and there is an unreasonable response. The reason that the word 'innocent' so often appears before the word 'bystanders' is that such witnesses to workplace bullying are already immersed in the culture which has created this situation but have not initiated it. Mary O' Neill:

> "Bullying arises where authority is weak, where there is poor management, where there is a lack of will to control the behaviour or a lack of understanding about the impact of bullying on others."

This is why bystanders must take recourse to company values instead of breathing in this foul atmosphere. Only then, and through stated and lived values, can they become immune to occurrences of bullying. Today, bystanders can do this by becoming what is known as an 'upstander'.

An upstander is a person who speaks or acts in support of an individual or cause — and it is a term which particularly applies to someone who intervenes on behalf of a person being attacked or bullied. One thing that good upstanders do, for example, is stop untrue and malicious information from spreading. That is to say, if you hear some unhelpful or unpleasant gossip and consciously decide not to repeat it or join in in any way, you are upstanding instead of bystanding. Upstanders are also welcoming when it comes to new people in the workplace, and this is important because starting a new job can be difficult and is always a challenge for the person who is new. That is why friendly upstanders are so important.

There are plenty more active routes to upstanding than this. You might want to convene a meeting to talk about bullying behaviour, for example, even if there is no suggestion of such a thing at that point. That is what an upstander would do. Bullying behaviour relies on people's difficulty to discuss it, and where it is not acknowledged, it thrives. Simply talking about bullying behaviour reduces the chances of it happening, and such a meeting will reassure everyone in the workgroup that everyone else is in agreement that certain behaviours — the behaviours we define as bullying — are unacceptable.

Upstanders are therefore always courageous, action-oriented and compassionate — all positive and infectious qualities.

Upstanding is not for everyone. While noble in principal, such actions as described here can sometimes be ineffective, especially if there is a powerful individual leveraging their status or aggression, nearby. Think of Hollywood's most iconic moment of upstanding, from the 1960 film *Spartacus*. There is a point in that movie when the bullying Romans try to locate the rebel leader by offering a pardon if the defiant slave army will identify Spartacus. In a dramatic upstanding against oppression, every man responds by shouting "I am Spartacus!" It is a powerful moment but as a result of their display of solidarity, every upstanding one of them is sentenced to death by crucifixion. So upstanding is a not a risk-free process!

While upstanding is always the right thing to do, it still requires courage. Internet searching the term 'upstander' does reveal a surplus of optimistic web pages encouraging us all to intervene in bullying when we see it — but upstanding is certainly one of these things where 'easier said than done' applies. So, to make upstanding safe and to avoid any unintended crucifixions, there are a few steps we can all take.

First, have a short chat with yourself (or someone else) before you carry out any positive interventions. Remember that upstanding is not an end goal and nor is it a definitive state of being. Upstanding is a set of ideals we can aspire to and a general direction to be heading in, rather than a fixed behaviour. It is also a response to circumstances, and so it is helpful if upstanders are aware of bullying behaviours, and clear about identifying them.

Next, be realistic about what you can achieve in any

upstanding intervention, and once you have achieved it, then withdraw and review the situation. Once more this is to keep you safe. If you are brave enough to intervene when someone is being bullied, you are going out on a limb — and limbs can break easily.

In discussing the types of workplace we want to build, we require role-modelled behaviour, most especially from managers and business owners. So many of these individuals feel that certain commonly shared values do not apply to them, and for reasons of their own they behave as if they are a law unto themselves. This is why it's important to call meetings at which values are discussed, so that such managers and owners eventually all get the idea that the values of the workplace are common to everybody, and apply to everybody.

It can be challenging to recognise right from wrong in an situation that is volatile and unfolding, and because bullying can often be relational and covert, upstanders must remember that not everything is how it seems.

That's why it's worth taking the time to be clear about what you are trying to achieve as an upstander and always refer to values such as respect, in an effort to move participants out of danger areas and on to safer ground.

To ensure that upstanding behaviour is a viable option in a workplace, and that other bullying prevention efforts are successful, it is best that staff are trained on what constitutes bullying behaviour, and what the workplace's policies are.

All that is required here is that we talk about bullying and are frank when we think we see it. There are successful routes out of this maze but there are also paths which lead to darker and more dangerous areas. While naming and shaming suspected bullies is unhelpful and can lead us into to deeper trouble, befriending someone who is threatened will work wonders, because workers who are bullied and who have a caring friend are less likely to develop health problems as a result of any trauma.

And even better, those who bully others can also benefit from restorative practices that help them to acknowledge their aggressive behaviour and work toward positive change.

ANTI-BULLY, INC.

The more we learn about bullying behaviour,
the closer we get to working here.
Welcome to ANTI-BULLY, INC.

BULLYTAINMENT

This is the promotional invective, delivered by Lord Alan Sugar, which introduces the British version of the long-running television programme, *The Apprentice*:

> "I want winners — not whingers! Workers — not shirkers!"

Sounds a bit like bullying? The show — essentially a reality format TV with a business twist — features a group of aspiring businesspeople competing to win a cash prize and personal mentoring offered by the business magnate, Lord Alan Sugar.

The contestants are frequently embroiled in personal and professional conflicts, with Lord Sugar cast as adjudicator alongside trusted (and now profiled) business lieutenants. There's plentiful pantomime here. The fighting, backbiting, jealousies and, on many occasions, the ineptitude of the contestants fuel the programme's popularity, not just in the UK but as part of a worldwide franchise.

By contracting 'bullying' and 'entertainment' we get

'bullytainment'. With caveats, *The Apprentice* looks and feels like a case study in just that. Indeed, the show can be viewed as a form of curated bullying.

Would such a show be of interest if it featured a group of reasonable and considerate participants, who were realistic about their capabilities, while being judged by a calm and benevolent businessman?

Unlikely. Instead, the stresses and fighting are initiated by the hothouse environment in which the candidates are placed, and driven by the host, who uses abrasive language and thinks little of insulting participants before each other and the watching world.

Productions like *The Apprentice* show us how not to behave and are a form of methodised bullying. Yes — what we see in shows like this are bullying behaviours, but this is not the same as witnessing bullying. The players are complicit — they've 'signed up'.

Bullying is not occurring in a situation where everybody is aware of what is going on. Bullying isn't taking place where the caustic language and behaviour is carried out with advisers and even therapists on hand, should anybody get upset for real. And bullying cannot occur where values such as safety and consideration are present and acted upon.

Could there be an element of catharsis or even education for the audience in this? Is it almost therapy?

The brutality that runs through the programme is summed up succinctly by Lord Sugar, addressing contestants:

> "If you're unhappy with my process, you can go and tell it to my HR firm: 'Diddums and Don't Care'."

Then there's the softer Lord Sugar. Here he is coming to the defence of contestants who were criticised by the public for making too many basic mistakes. He said:

> "The program itself is an entertainment program as well as a business program. Those 'stupid' people you're talking about run six very successful businesses, one of which has made a million pounds this year." (Huffington Post UK 25.09.2018)

The Apprentice is unlike certain other 'bullytainment' shows, because contestants are not explicitly asked to do anything humiliating strictly for the sake of the viewer's fun.

In fact, in *The Apprentice* the participants are asked to perform reasonable tasks using common sense and creativity — unlike in another example of bullytainment, *I'm A Celebrity... Get Me Out of Here!* In *I'm a Celebrity...* the contestants are obliged, among other unpleasant activities, to eat live insects.

While both these shows are consensual and may show bullying behaviour (as differentiated from intentional bullying) contestants in *The Apprentice* are bullied in other ways. They are for example subject to early morning wake-up calls (5.30am anyone?) and often shown in the worst possible light. Viewers are, for example, far more likely to see their disagreements and hysterics, than they are their helpful co-operation. Then there is the fact that the contestants are usually talked down to as "boys and girls" as opposed to "men and women" by Lord Sugar. Similarly, a dismissive "Off you go" is the standard Lord Sugar phrase to kick start each programme.

Viewers know that the participants are there by consent and yet there is an ongoing undertone of oppression, which can as we all know drive — but not fully explain — erratic and anxious behaviour, as well as underachievement.

It's interesting how targets of real-life workplace bullying react to *The Apprentice*. For some, the show is a reminder of the premeditated desire and calculated intention to hurt that they have witnessed in their own bullying experiences. *The Apprentice* shows us the plausible damage that can be done by framing bullying in a certain light. Lord Sugar addressed this himself in 2014:

> "It is not bullying to speak your mind. I don't flower my words. If someone is useless, I'll tell them. If someone has done a good job, I'll also tell them. Identifying a truth is not bullying ... No one likes to be told a home truth." (The Guardian 07.10.2014)

This is an imperious and absolute view of what a workplace should be and doesn't take into account any system of values, other than those that may apply in such dictatorial environments, where Darwinian rules apply.

And while it is true that "identifying a truth is not bullying," there is much to be said about the delivery of that truth. Shout it at someone and call them 'rubbish', then Lord Sugar is wrong, because that is bullying behaviour. Call a meeting and present the truth calmly, objectively within the framework of a constructive outcome, and it is not.

While this curated vision of bullying is something most people can enjoy in relative comfort, assured that what they are watching is not in any important sense real, it is not quite the same as the regular feed we as bystanders receive of celebrity stories, many of which fall into much more traditional modes of bullying.

Widespread bullying by social media users is increasingly common with examples emerging almost daily, as in the case of comedian Pete Davidson, who said that he was bullied online for months after his split with singer and actress Ariana Grande (bbc.co.uk 03.12.2018). In this case, Davidson was pursued by 'Stan' fans (the term inspired by the Eminem track 'Stan') — overzealous followers of Ms Grande. Davidson claimed further fall-out from his experience by drawing attention to how his mother — a school nurse — was bullied at her workplace by fans of Ms Grande singing her song 'Thank U, Next' at her — the song itself about moving on from the relationship.

Celebrities, and almost exclusively women, are particularly vulnerable to mass abuse from people who might not ordinarily call names in real life, but who become members of social media mobs.

Melania Trump claimed on ABC Tonite that she was no stranger to bullying, given the ongoing hostility she faces online, saying: "I could say that I'm the most bullied person in the world" (11.10.2018).

BBC Radio presenter Jo Whiley spoke of the bullying behaviour she faced when she was parachuted into a Radio 2 drive-time slot with male colleague Simon Mayo. There were accusations of tokenism. Crucially, those unhappy with Ms Wiley's addition to the show took to social media, specifically Twitter to share their feelings. In an interview with the Daily Mail she described the abuse she received as 'savage' and told how this orchestrated criticism had 'chipped away' at her, adding "aside from family dramas, this is the toughest thing I've had to endure."

Journalist Cathy Newman was the target of substantial aggression and abuse after her interview with Canadian psychologist Jordan Petersen; and British diver Tom Daly is still subject to homophobic abuse and other bullying, not just when he competes, but even if he is in the news for other reasons. This online mobbing of celebrities is an ongoing global phenomenon, it seems, and it never takes a break. Politicians are subject to it too, and you don't even have to be in the mainstream media to attract a mob. No sphere is safe.

It is also troubling when media outlets use their own reach to bully celebrities, either to generate sales or for what looks like simple malice. The attack on British TV personality and campaigner Stacey Solomon in 2018, by Now magazine is a particularly uncomfortable example.

How do we know this is bullying? The magazine described Solomon as 'Boring, Desperate and Cheap' — not within its pages but in large capital letters on its the cover. Stacey Solomon herself called the attack "the meanest thing I've ever seen" (Twitter 28.08.2018) and given the venom and crudity of the message, it's hard not to agree with her.

Startlingly, the open aggression in the magazine headline made its readers into complicit bystanders. Judging by responses to Ms Solomon's own Twitter account, many were horrified and angry on her behalf, while others seemed to enjoy the outpourings of upset and rage — including the heart-broken reaction from the target, who described herself as "hurt" and movingly "not a robot".

Solomon had to pick up the pieces and find the strength

to lead the defence. While her fans were ready to support her, it is possible that virtually nothing would have happened if Stacey Solomon had not chosen to fight back. It's a reminder that what bullies crave is that the target lie down and die, or effectively 'go and eat worms'.

The song is as ever apt. It is the attack on the self-confidence of the target that makes bullying what it is. It is the assertion that not only the bully does not like the target, but that nobody does. The publishers of Now, TI Media, seem to have aimed at as wide a slur as possible here, by trying to imply that it was their whole readership who were passing judgement, and not themselves.

The other point that stands out in this example is that, as with many cases of bullying, the bystanding public lost interest pretty quickly.

While that is in the nature of the news media, it is far from certain that Stacey Solomon will ever forget that magazine cover. Although an apology was issued from Now, the concession made by the magazine was rejected by Stacey Solomon, and reading it, you can see why.

The apology read:

> "The story featured in this week's issue of Now Magazine regarding Stacey Solomon was written on the basis of social media comments about Stacey and is not the opinion of Now Magazine. As a publication, we simply aim to inspire debate amongst our readers about their favourite celebrities and TV stars, including Stacey. We do not encourage or condone bullying in any form. We apologise to Stacey for any distress our story may have caused." (Daily Mail 30.08.2018)

This apology reeks of insincerity. The stand-out aspects of this 'fake' apology are recognisable, and targets and bystanders alike should watch out for this sort of thing and learn to recognise what is a real apology and what is not. In this case, not only is the blame passed to 'social media', but the magazine's editors, disingenuously in our opinion, state that in repeating malicious comments that others have made, they are merely fomenting debate. The editors are even ridiculously on the verge of suggesting they're doing a public service, compounding the initial insults. Finally, and perhaps most insultingly, the editors who made the purposeful and conscious decision to distress Stacey Solomon offer a classic fake excuse — saying that it was 'the story' that hurt her, and not their behaviour.

Targets of bullying will identify with this, especially if they have received statements to the effect that it was not a person that bullied them — but instead it was an environment — or that it was an attitude — or a situation.

For this reason, Stacey Solomon was correct to reject this apology. Reading it, you can almost hear the sniggering editors at work behind this artfully insincere statement.

'Bullytainment' doesn't look like it's going away. Such curated 'bullying as entertainment' is just about permissible in carefully orchestrated and regulated environments and with pre-consent. But if it means mercilessly targeting individuals — be it at work or online — and implying negative values then, fairly obviously, not.

With social media so often the driver, reversing this trend is going to be challenging. Celebrities are a special case. Not only is it us that made them what they are, but they are virtually always 'at work', one way or another. When celebrities are out in public, they are at work, just as they are at work when we read about them and when they are interviewed. Their workplaces are not just studios and film-sets. Their very workplace is the media that they support.

Arguably celebrity and its voracious consumption by media and by extension, ourselves, has just had its #MeToo epiphany.

Because much as the sport of targeting celebs is part and parcel of our media — the clicks, the views, the rankings and the revenues — something has started to go wrong. Dramatically so. A media which has an appetite for photographing women celebs getting out of cars — an example of 'wardrobe malfunction' as they call it — is not overly exercised by the concept of taste. In 2019, TV presenter Lorraine Kelly found out that the act of crossing her legs was something that generated content online and in print for The Mirror, and she was not alone.

Is this bullytainment? Yes, if it's quantified as demeaning.

Still, the scope of what bullytainment entails has been dramatically altered. Perhaps permanently.

This shape-shifting was triggered by the tragic death of Jack Saunders, 25, a contestant on the TV juggernaut that is ITV's *Britain's Got Talent*. Jack took his own life prior to a semi-final appearance on the show with his dance troupe, Green Force Five.

The link between this young man's death and being part of the reality TV treadmill — he'd also appeared on *X Factor* and Sky One's *Got To Dance* — is visible.

His is not an isolated case. Globally, it is said that some 38 performers have committed suicide after going through the reality TV wringer. In the UK the series *Love Island* — a voyeuristic format where hyper attractive young people are plonked on an island while we watch nature and hormones take their course — lost two of its contestants to suicide. Sophie Gradon, 32, took her own life in June 2018; while 26-year-old Mike Thalassitis did the same in March of 2019, following the death of his grandmother.

One of Sophie's co-stars in *Love Island*, Malin Andersson, focused on the need for producers to provide "better after-care" once their reality TV show window has closed. This issue of after-care is paramount. Because plunging people ill-equipped to deal with the vagaries of fame — hot one day, nobody the next, the orchestrated hate pouring out of social media, and so forth — is a dangerous game. People's lives are literally at stake.

In an unprecedented step, the producers of *Love Island* made a public statement following Mike's death. They addressed the issue of after-care and the vague and at times dangerous space that celebs or nearly-celebs occupy after the intense attention stage has been gone through. When the cameras have stopped whirring and when normal life kicks in once again.

That is significant in itself because most PRs would have advised the programme's producers to say nothing. They could have ridden it out. But they didn't. This is what they had to say:

> "Care for our islanders is a process the show takes very seriously and is a continuous process for all those taking part in the show. We ensure that all of our contributors are able to access psychological support

> before, during and after appearing on the show. The programme will always provide ongoing support when needed and where appropriate. We also discuss at length with all of our islanders, before and after the show, how their lives might change, and they have access to support and advice to help with this."

Additionally, however, TV chief executive Carolyn McCall was quoted in The Evening Standard (28.03.2019) as saying that ITV does "everything it can" for contestants following the show, but that this must end somewhere. The ITV boss drew a clear line in the sand regarding what she felt were the channel's responsibilities, adding:

> "I would also say that I don't think anybody has made a direct link between what happened to Mike and *Love Island*. That would be an extremely tenuous thing to do given he was very happy on *Love Island* and all his mates have said that, and he's done two other reality programmes since then. We can do everything we possibly can to look after people and to do our duty of care, but you can't do that forever with an individual. There has got to be a framework and it will come to an end. It can't be indefinite."

Regardless of that, and in spite of the deaths, 60,000 people applied to be on the following series of *Love Island*.

And the show had far worse in store, when only months later, on February 15th 2020, and aged 40, Caroline Flack a *Love Island* presenter also took her own life. Following her death, a petition was launched calling for new laws to prevent sections of the media 'knowingly and relentlessly bullying people, famous or not'.

For sure, the way that certain media outlets changed their tune following Caroline Flack's death suggested that they felt a degree of responsibility. The morning before Caroline died, The Sun newspaper had led with a brutal Valentine's Day card mocking her. Shortly after her death was announced, this was taken offline and replaced with a message concerning the paper's 'You're Not Alone' suicide prevention campaign, first launched in 2018.

Then there is The Mirror, which switched from (for example) 'expert' body language testimony presenting their target as 'dead-eyed' in January, when they were reporting on every lurid detail of her domestic life and assault charges — to calling her 'inspirational' in February, when she was dead.

The Sun however, will be be watched more closely than ever, although they look unlikely to take any responsibility for their part in Caroline's suicide. This is the newspaper that two months previously had obtained exclusive pictures of the star's bloodied bedroom after an alleged domestic assault. As well as blaming another media outlet (ITV, the producers of *Love Island*) and The Crown Prosecution Service, The Sun did not publicly attack that other potentially guilty party — ourselves. As Jim Waterson, Media Editor of The Guardian said following the death:

> "Individuals who work at leading British tabloids privately pointed out on Sunday that many of the people now criticising press intrusion into Flack's life

> were likely to have been among the millions of readers who had previously rushed to click on articles about the presenter's arrest in December for allegedly assaulting her boyfriend." (The Guardian 15.02.2020)

The successful petition which followed Caroline Flack's death and which gathered over one million signatures in two days, sought to establish laws against 'intrusion' by media companies, and was spot on when it mentioned bullying in its text. There is a definite element of bullying involved in this type of coverage. This can be anything from outright denigration, and sensational speculation, to the widespread repetition of slurs from multiple sources, thus creating social media mobs. Caroline had already described this process herself in her 2015 autobiography, in which she described what happened when the press discovered she was dating a man 14 years her junior. "It was open season," she wrote. "After that anyone could say anything. In the street people started shouting at me 'paedophile' and 'pervert'."

In 2019, things really did begin to come to a head regarding this form of entertainment, in Great Britain at least, where for many years Jeremy Kyle specialised in high octane, confrontational telly. It was a simple formula in which a live studio audience became embroiled in the life stories of guests and effectively cheerlead and vilified as it saw fit. These shows were meticulously staged and pre-warm up, the audience were directed as to how they should behave. In 2019 however, and having run since 2005, The Jeremy Kyle Show was taken off air along with its online archive.

The reason? A guest — Steve Dymond, 63 — failed the

show's heavily staged 'lie detector' test. A vulnerable soul by some accounts, he took his own life a week after filming for the show in which the issue was his fidelity. He failed the test and on that basis the ending of his relationship followed swiftly.

Did the show sow the seeds for this? Absolutely. And the larger picture is also clear: all of a sudden it is not uncommon for television — and our appetite for reality based entertainment — to be implicated in the death of a guest or celebrity. Despite a lot of hand wringing and TV producers expressing regret, it seems clear that the duty of care owed to guests, and others, is inadequate.

It's a dangerous formula: TV as confessional. And after those 15 minutes of fame and exposure, guests can be left high and dry. No one is suggesting that every reality show should offer unending support to all guests, and even hosts. But vetting them properly in the first place and toning down the lynch mob mentality of the audience would help. Less whooping, more caring.

It's clear that the whole selection (or curation?) process on reality TV needs to be seriously rethought, now that a line can be drawn between appearance and self-harm and in extreme cases death. In 2019, Caroline Wharram, a former *Big Brother* contestant, shared her experience of her interactions with the show's producers. She described herself to the Daily Mail as having been "an anxious, lonely and sad young girl with a crippling eating disorder and a family history of mental health problems".

Yet she walked through the psychological assessments required to appear on the show.

What did she make of that?

> "I can only conclude that the producers just didn't care as long as I was entertaining". Adding: "In my view the programme makers had little interest in assessing my mental suitability. They failed, for example, to ask me a single question about any mental health problems I might have had."

A contentious segment featuring Caroline behaving in an eccentric way was repeated often in show promos. And an offensive comment that she made about another contestant — which she now disowns as "thoughtless" — gave the producers what they wanted: water cooler moments, and ones that heated up ratings. Let's not forget: the producers are gods in this context, and that the choices are theirs.

Pamela Anderson, a veteran of reality shows as well as iconic 90s hit *Baywatch*, is clear on how she feels about reality TV, describing it as an "epidemic of ugliness".

She told The Mirror:

> "You are usually bullied into doing TV like this by agents fighting over commissions. You're left without any great amount of joy or money. You feel used, dirty, and with no feeling of accomplishment."

See? It's that word 'bullied' again, and from someone who has been through the celeb mill for years. Pamela Anderson has a solution however: stop them being made. She says: "Please no more reality shows or reality stars…. It's an epidemic of ugliness, superficial competitions, desperate and exploitative for the artist."

Reality, and any curated or incidental bullying that goes with it, is now a staple for TV companies, however. Will they really be able to give it up?

We doubt it. Ted Coiné:

> "I watched a couple of minutes of *Survivor* in its first season and realised that this kind of TV isn't for me. Maybe it shouldn't be for anyone — it's only entertaining if it's hurtful. While I have trouble feeling sorry for contestants — by now they know what they're signing up for — the entire industry is like an emotional Circus Maximus. It's terrible for society.
>
> "Since late 2015, I've been thinking a lot about where our entertainment technology has brought us. Our society is suffering self-inflicted degradation from a toxic triumvirate: 24/7 news channels, reality TV, and social media. As author of a book extolling the virtues of *A World Gone Social*, I hate to say how wrong I was, focusing at the democratising benefits of social media while ignoring the poison inherent in the very same platforms. That book appeared in 2014 and we were so focused on the business aspect of social, especially regarding the newly empowered customer (as brand advocate or assassin), that we completely ignored the political horror show that social media, has enabled.
>
> "If I could wave a magic wand and make something disappear for the betterment of humanity, it would be that toxic triumvirate. Sadly, I think the genie is out of the bottle, and it's not going back in."

VALUE-ADDED WORKPLACES

Knowing what our values are can help us make consistent decisions that we are happy with. Once we understand what our values are, decision making will be easier. Further, when you know what someone else's values are, you can anticipate their decision making too — and if you don't know what your company's values are, then those values can become the values of the biggest autocratic bully in the room.

Some say that happened in the case of the US presidency on January 17 2017. It happens in families and it happens in schools, and it certainly happens at work. Later, we always wonder the same thing: how did we allow this bully to get so far?

The answer to this is easier to formulate in retrospect, but it tends to boil down to the fact that the angry autocrats get away with what they do because others allow it to happen. In a tech start-up I spoke to, in which bullying was rife, one business owner ended up managing issues through a combination of angry dressing downs, sackings and by shrouding a lot of the business' activity in secrecy. There had never once been any discussion of values at this company and so decision making tended be based on the attitude, ideals and scruples of that one business owner. As a consequence, everyone suffered — even the clients of that business.

When we use the word 'values' in considering a business or workplace, what we specifically mean are (abstract) shared organisational goals.

These values can be reached collectively by staff and can create a bully-free workplace. I would go so far as to state that knowing and observing your company values will create bully-free habits in all areas of the business. What this boils down to is employee engagement — a belief in connecting with people's emotions at work, by having a value-driven team or organisation.

I'd present a value as something to which we can aspire. Unlike material items to which we aspire, a value will be an abstract.

To give an example, 'money' could not be considered to be a value because it is something tangible. The acquisition of money could however be considered a good thing if it allows you or your company to aspire to a value such as 'security', or 'fun'. So if 'security' is a stated value, then by all means acquiring money can be seen as a positive because the money, when obtained, will afford this value. The same can be said of 'fun'. If 'fun' is a value, then making money can facilitate this.

Many healthily functioning organisations are now public about their values. Practically speaking this is akin to a moral technology that will increase happiness at work and protect against the health risks associated with bullying behaviour. The Cyrenians, a Scottish charity working to end homelessness and support vulnerable people, have stated that their values are as follows: Respect, Compassion, Innovation and Integrity. At a school I visited I observed that the school's values were similar, and included: Responsibility, Grace, Enthusiasm and Kindness. What was marvellous about this school was that these values were displayed in every single room on the premises — over 250 times.

Values are still abstract, and even if seeing them written down serves as a check for personnel, they don't do a lot of good placed on a poster on the wall. Group values need to be discussed on some kind of regular basis so that people feel confident about using them to inform behaviour, company decisions, and decisions made by individuals. Finally, the values need to be demonstrated, and to be seen in practice. Where this type of model comes into its own is in making sure that these values do not simply remain as words which everyone nods to now and then. Instead, the values are constantly viewed, reviewed, and discussed.

Should you as a manger or as a company be in any doubt as to what potential values may look like, consider these following examples. All of these are abstract values to which a person or an organisation may aspire. All of these values can be used to lead decision making, and it is of course up to each company to decide which values they wish to follow.

Some example might be: authenticity — achievement — compassion — citizenship — community — competence — creativity — fairness — faith — fun — growth — justice — learning — openness — optimism — recognition — reputation — respect — safety — service — trustworthiness — wisdom.

All of these values are positive and they represent aspirations. What is so effective about working with aspirational values such as these is that the aspiration can often be achieved. One of the reasons that so many new companies go out of business is because a lack of preparation in this area. In business, new situations arise all the time, and leaving the decision making to the 'vision' of the company founder isn't always the right thing to do, especially if the company founder is the angry, ignorant or domineering sort!

Instead, truly visionary managers and company owners approach the future armed with stated values, prepared to look at every single aspect of the company in the light of these. That includes their own behaviour.

Unpopular culture is full of tales of angry business owners. One such is the story of Sir Philip Green the British businessman, and the chairman of a retail group that includes Topshop, Topman, Wallis, Evans, Burton, Miss Selfridge, Dorothy Perkins and Outfit. Another might be CEO of Ted Baker, Ray Kelvin. Both men appear to have been individuals who felt that they were able to make the law in their places of work, and that generally held company values did not apply to them. This is something that can happen anywhere. You do not need to own a chain of shops to be such a bully as these men were accused of being — you could own one or two shops and be the same.

The common factor is that you see yourself as the one in charge and the one who makes the rules. The common factor is that you target those who don't fit in with your plans, and fear no consequences in doing so. Being trapped in a working relationship with people like this is disastrous and life-changing for the worse.

If your company, workspace or team is not working on behalf of a plan of values, then nobody will know what to do when either success or failure looms. And if you are not working on behalf of a plan of values, then individuals within your team may find themselves lost in errors of decision making, or worse, starting to impose their own values.

Finally, if you don't know what your company or your workgroup's values are then how can you even measure its success? It isn't all about the bottom line. After all, anyone can bully their way to a profit. It happens all the time.

It is therefore always helpful to know what your company or workgroup's values are. Some values may be more applicable for certain workplaces, and all may equally apply. The important thing is that you don't just stick these values on a noticeboard and get back to work. Your team needs to meet every so often to discuss the various ways in which you are living up to the values, or if need be, how you are failing to do so. This is because values are there, like it or not — and if you don't actively pick a set of positive values, you may well end up dancing to the tune of a set of negative ones.

Some large brands today are progressive enough to state their values online. All of the following values have been sourced from the relevant organisations' websites and were accurate at the time of publication. The following are only examples, and do not represent comprehensive lists of any of the following company's core objectives or ethics. These values which follow are cherry-picked from a few different sources and intended to offer readers an idea of what company values look like and how they might work:

Facebook lists 'democracy' as one its core values. This must be helpful in decision making, allowing anyone in the company to ask: "was that decision democratically achieved?" In November 2018, a story originating in the New York Times suggested that because of a row over privacy, Facebook 'banned its management team from using Apple-made smartphones.' (The Sun 16.11.2018). It was reported that this decision came from the Facebook CEO, and if this was true, surely the act was more suggestive of autocracy than democracy — and as such would be apparent to all employees as a possible failing.

Apple have cited 'simplicity' as a value. This idea clearly guides Apple's design ethos, but I'm sure it also applies to their management styles, achieving something that is strong and easily understood. 'Simplicity' isn't the most immediately obvious example of a value, but it certainly must help when it comes to preferences, compromises and other aspects of management.

Delta Airlines lists 'honesty' and 'integrity' among its five core values. This is interesting because for many of us the two might seem to be the same thing. For Delta 'honesty' and 'integrity' are not the same thing however, and they explain this as follows: 'Always tell the truth – Honesty' and 'Always keep your deals – Integrity'.

One of **Google**'s core values is that a company can still make money without 'doing evil'. One of the ways Google argue that they act on this value, is by serving relevant and non-manipulative adverts to their web users.

Finally, the **Constitution of the United States** asserts that 'justice' is a value of the US government. This allows a simple question to be asked at every stage in every decision-making process that the government tackles: 'Is this just?' While not every decision that is made may in the end be found to be just, what is provided here is a benchmark by which to evaluate these decisions.

Core values are something which an organisation holds constantly. Such values are not usually consciously created but become a part of the company, likely as a result of the views of the company's founders. If this is true, and values are discovered and not invented, then imagine what a company run by a bully is going to have as its values.

It may not be a very happy company at all — first because staff will be unsure of what to expect (stated values could fix this!) and because the company will be run on the basis of one person's whims.

Some company owners beg to differ and will argue that as the company belongs to them, they can do as they please. For these business owners and bosses, staff are paid to take instruction and sometimes there isn't much more to working life than that. Staff in these environments can often grow to feel undervalued and unhappy. In light of this, values can and will accentuate bullying behaviour. A value will be a check on everybody — but because of their autocratic nature, this is why bullies invariably avoid this discussion, or argue that it is either nonsensical or not appropriate to introduce airy-fairy values. Such a business owner or manager will argue something along the lines of: "I don't have to explain myself and my decisions to you."

If you have heard that line at your place of work, then welcome to BULLY, INC. You now know that for the best results — and that includes a happy, bully-free working environment — companies should consider their values.

This isn't just applicable to new companies, but it works for companies that have been running for some time. Do bear in mind that it is never too late to discuss values at work and that anybody at any point can establish what their values are, or what they would like them to be. I can guarantee that any organisation or workgroup that carries out this exercise and finds out what their values are, and monitors them on a six-monthly basis, will see their business flourish. Values evolve, sometimes unnoticed, and listing them is never a waste of time. Once values have been identified, this is when they can be acted upon and used as guiding factors in troubled times.

At the tech start-up I described above, there were values — but they were not healthy values. At that company, it appeared that secrecy was a value, because so much of what went on happened on a need-to-know basis. This was as simple as staff being told what to do, and never truly informed why they had to do it. Some people were paid different amounts to others, for no good reason, and when an ambush meeting occurred and one manager intimidated another manager (emotional abuse), this remained a complete secret. The rest of the company knew that something grave had happened, but nobody was told what went on, or why it went on.

Another value at this company, it appears, was fear, including a common fear of making mistakes. Sadly, this fear of making mistakes translated itself into people actually making more mistakes, and over a period of months, people were sacked when in fact a performance review would have been more appropriate.

Another unhelpful value at this tech start-up was control. As the management style was one of control, this filtered down through the group so that everybody became possessive about what was theirs to manage and consequently rather uncaring about what was not theirs to manage. The most unpleasant workaday manifestation of this was people being told that a certain thing — such as the dismissal of another staff member — was none of their business.

Although these values were apparent, they were never codified. The values were apparent because they could be seen as a guiding influence on company decisions and actions. Nobody however starts a company and dedicates that company to following such values. This fact alone should be proof enough of the effectiveness of dedicating your company to a set of positive values.

In the case of the cosmetics firm Lush, detailed later, we can see that the happiness of staff is considered as a stated value. This is something that was never mentioned at this rather dysfunctional tech start-up, and in fact, unhappy staff were encouraged to leave — effectively bullied out of the door. It's quite a thought, but look around and listen to others, and you will see it's not so uncommon for things to be run that way.

Let us go into the future workplace then — the workplace in which external values guide and advise us — and where bullying behaviour can be choked out of existence, for lack of a foothold.

SNOWFLAKE VERSUS BULLY?

Why do millennials consistently receive such woeful press? Every internet search of the word 'millennial' returns a pre-formed syntax of negativity: the millennials are 'snowflakes' — they are 'delusional', 'lazy' and 'coddled' — all expressions presented in an influential article on the subject in TIME magazine, May 2013, titled 'The Me Me Me Generation'.

The title of this article sums up the unenthusiastic attitude which seems to prevail regarding this generation. Like other commentators, the author presents clichés that seem to have worked their way into our belief system, including the infamous millennial 'sense of entitlement' — the compulsive job-hopping — the notion that millennials supposedly have little time for their more experienced colleagues — and the idea that millennials are likely to have been brought up to have unrealistic expectations concerning life and most particularly, work.

In fact, millennials have been called the 'Peter Pan' or 'Boomerang' generation because of a perceived tendency they have to move back in with their parents.

This may be due to economic constraints, but it is also

put down to a belief that this cohort, which numbers about 85 million people in the US workforce, and about 18 million in the UK workforce, have chosen to delay some of the traditional adulthood rites of passage like marriage or starting a career.

The media have nothing positive to say about this generation — those born between 1981 and 1996 — with 'narcissistic' being a keyword.

In the workforce, millennials are often held to be lazy and prone to jump from job to job. In his book *Trophy Kids* (2008), Ron Alsop argues that (much of) this may be because many millennials were rewarded for relatively modest or basic accomplishments (including mere participation) and that their parents and educators tended to encourage them away from traditionally competitive attitudes, to focus on rights, values and other abstracts.

In brief, the argument runs that as a result of their upbringing and schooling, millennials have unrealistic expectations of working life.

This is one of these instances in which a series of broad assertions become a narrative. The theme of the meandering millennial has in fact become a trope, exacerbated by movies like *Lost in Translation* (2003) and presented as fully formed lifestyle-cum-corporate entity in *The Social Network* (2010), the story of the ultimate millennial, Facebook founder Mark Zuckerberg.

The trouble with these narratives is that when they lie unquestioned, they grow out of control, and before we know it, lies have become a truth.

This happened in January 2019 when the British Army ran a recruiting campaign stating the following:

• "Me me me millennials, your army needs you and your self-belief."

And:

• "Snowflakes: your army needs you and your compassion."

The campaign used the same demeaning and fault-finding language that has been a feature of our discourse for a decade now, coupled with the suggestion that what millennials are being told are their weaknesses are somehow their virtues. Even if this advertising campaign thought it was doing a good thing by reaching out with encouraging arms, all it actually managed to do was underline our society's lack of faith in an entire generation, by reinforcing a trope.

It might be the case that older bosses and company owners are resistant to the thought of younger people having ideas. Bear in mind that anyone over 45 years of age was almost certainly brought up in an era of straightforward hierarchies. Specifically, company owners and managers in environments where bullying may now be embedded in the culture, will want staff to do as they ask, and treat any questions concerning the value of any role or task as interference.

Those same managers may in their time have been employed in what were once called 'McJobs' — the term popularised by Douglas Coupland in his novel *Generation X* in 1991 — low paid and meaningless work which filled a gap or allowed people to pursue another passion.

It follows that these same managers and business owners may be unconsciously seeking workers who behave rather like machines and operate with the minimum of human needs. These same bosses are confused and irritated when their employees want more than just a job, but seek instead a lifestyle with a sense of values.

Millennials won't have it though — and this resistance is certainly no reason to call them lazy or privileged. In an important 2010 article on the subject, 'Meet The Millennials', Leigh Buchanan, a former editor at Harvard Business Review, wrote:

> "One of the characteristics of millennials, besides the fact that they are masters of digital communication, is that they are primed to do well by doing good. Almost 70% say that giving back and being civically engaged are their highest priorities."

What this suggests is that millennials don't have a problem with holding their own when asked to do something that goes against their values. This is bad news for bullies — because this generation won't buckle.

As with any new generation, older generations must adjust their needs and values. This should always be a positive process, but when bosses and older colleagues double down on rules that have served them well and ape the belief that the younger people are either entitled or self-interested, then this is fertile ground for bullying.

It's perfect ground for bullying in fact because it is a clash of culture, and so the older colleagues will not even see themselves as bullies. They will see themselves as knowing what is best and end up supporting an older form of hierarchy and what unfortunately turn out to be out-of-date practises.

This is how this entire 'millennial vocabulary' of entitlement and privilege has developed. It's happened because business owners and managers have reacted to millennials' requests — rather than respond to them.

Organisational consultant Simon Sinek tends to make light of this in his own studies of millennials in the workplace. Sinek characterises the millennials as wanting "free food and beanbags" at work (*Simon Sinek on Millennials in the Workplace*, YouTube, 2016), and when he talks, he covers many of the same repeated emblems of millennial life, including participation medals, high grades awarded without merit and children being told they were special and that they could do anything they wanted in life. It is Sinek's belief that this entire generation lacks self-esteem "through no fault of their own."

How? He suggests "they were dealt a bad hand."

In discussing a dopamine-fuelled, social-network driven world of instant gratification, Sinek is perhaps too dismissive, suggesting that as far as job satisfaction is concerned, that "there is no app for that." Job satisfaction is according to him a "slow, messy and uncomfortable process." He adds:

> "It's as if they (the millennials) are standing at the foot of the mountain and they have this abstract concept called 'impact' that they want to have in the world — which is the summit — but what they don't see is the mountain."

Sinek claims millennials need to learn patience. He points to statistics which suggest that suicide rates are higher among this generation, as are both dropping out of education and accidental deaths due to drug overdoses. The best he says this generation have to look forward to is that they will never find joy or fulfilment.

If it is true that our corporate environments are contributing to this by caring more about short-term gains than long term satisfaction(s), then it is entirely up to our managers, leaders and company owners to respond. They may respond as Sinek suggests by "teaching" this generation "the social skills they are missing out on." Sinek argues for example "there should be no cell phones in conference rooms — none — zero!" And these instructions continue for example to not taking phones to meals — and so on.

While Sinek has good ideas regarding communication, the emphasis is on instructing the millennials how to behave. In a way, it could be argued, he's weaponising social skills here and seeking to exert and sustain prevailing mores.

An easier route may be learning from millennial values, rather than trying to mold them. This doesn't mean agreeing with some of the principal assertions made about this generation but listening to them instead of placing obstacles and restrictions before them. It would mean the generation which employs the millennials engaging fully with them.

More workplaces are becoming wise to this. Some are finding out that the contributions of this generation exceed those of the generations that both preceded them and follow them. The difference lies in society's sluggishness when it comes to new ideas — especially if those ideas come from the young.

Millennials do it differently. They grew up learning how to figure things out for themselves, knowing that with the Internet and a network of friends who are only a message away they will find the answers they need. Some see this as a negative — something along the lines of 'Millennials don't respect their elder colleagues'.

But the reverse is true. If anything, millennials value the opportunity to teach skills to older colleagues as well as learn from them. Maybe that's tough for older to people to hear, because they are a generation that became used to following orders and learning slowly. But what was previously a one-way street, has now opened a new lane and communication is going to have to work in both directions.

One of the benefits of this two-directional communication will be a reduction in workplace bullying. In light of shared values — established across generations and applicable to all employees — such commonly accepted emotional abuse and mistreatment can become consigned to history. Not the accepted fact of life in the workplace it has been for years.

The changing climate millennials bring to the workplace is identified in a feature titled 'Millennials At Work' (The Guardian 15.03.2016). In the article, Chris Gale, a public sector auditor for Grant Thornton, aged 21 at the time, spoke of his experience of 'reverse mentoring'. He said:

> "For someone my age it's rare to be in a position where I'm sat down with a senior partner showing them how to develop their online profile, and I just don't think that kind of role reversal would have happened a few years ago."

This is well worth paying attention to because this generation that we are talking about here will soon be the world's business leaders, and in the coming decade they will make up over half of the workforce of the entire world. If these business leaders and workers come to maturity still believing what they've been told about their entitlement and narcissism, then it won't be a pretty place to be. What works now, and will work for the future, is a discussion with that generation.

And if you call them 'snowflakes' and if a dismissive public attitude is maintained concerning that generation, they may decide that it isn't worth their while investing in their work or in a company culture.

It is the millennials who are the investment, and in not listening to them we risk continuing to live in an outdated workplace. They already are the drivers of change.

The dinosaurs will soon be extinct.

THE WORKPLACE ACCORDING TO LUSH

Are any employers getting it right in the workplace? In terms of major businesses, Lush does. Lush is an ethical cosmetics retailer headquartered in the UK, but with outlets globally. The company was founded in 1995 by six co-founders — Mark Constantine, Mo Constantine, Liz Weir, Rowena Bird, Helen Ambrosen and Paul Greeves — and has been internationally successful not only in terms of transforming the beauty products market — where were bath bombs before Lush? — but also in terms of being acknowledged as a great place to work.

Lush were listed by jobs website Indeed as one of the UK's top 10 retail private sector employers in 2018. (CNBC 22.10.2018). Indeed's list was compiled using data from hundreds of thousands of employee reviews and included both British and overseas-based firms. Lush are listed at number two — just behind John Lewis (established 1929).

Lush feel like a thoroughly modern company and a part of its success has been down to meeting its stated company values, which concentrate on ethical and inventive products, a happy staff and working environment, and offering value to customers — while at the same time maintaining profitability and growth.

In terms of values, Lush have excelled. Their website Lush.com features a variety of policies ranging from ethical buying, an ethical company tax policy, statements on external auditing, whistleblowing and charitable policies, as well as statements on customer experience, environmental policy and legal compliance. The company's values are prominently flagged on their website and deeply embedded in its business DNA. Significant because Lush is very much a public-facing company. It wants — as we found out — to talk, and share. Lush feels proud of its culture, values and dynamism.

Lush has been able to generate spectacular growth. Last audited figures showed total brand turnover at £987.4 million and the company was profiled in Forbes magazine as recently as 2017 in a piece headlined 'Taking The Industry By Storm.'

Lush's company culture not only gives everyone involved in the company something to live up to, it sends a positive message to the outside world.

Lush's values look like this: (Full text at uk.Lush.com/article/Lush-life-we-believe)

- Lush believe in inventing their own products from fresh, organic, top quality and safe materials;
- They are open and ethical about their manufacture;
- They state that they wish their staff to be happy;
- They believe in 'the right to make mistakes, lose everything and start again'.
- They believe in freedom of movement of people;

• Finally, Lush believe in good value, profit, and the fact that the customer is always right.

Note that value and profit are included, and that it's acceptable to state that your company seeks to make a profit, if that is one of its goals. Profit is an enabler — not the sole measure of success, but will allow your company to meet values that are going to require profits to achieve. The ethical values which are a constant and visible with Lush have generated an overwhelming and deep trust with consumers — who know what to expect from the company, in terms of standards both in manufacture and service.

Of these values, one that is usually missing from less optimised working environments is 'the right to make mistakes'. Both risk and failure challenge us all as human beings, and building trust between management and staff is not something that happens automatically. Stating to both staff and public that they acknowledge this, Lush have found a way to let all employees grow and permitted people and their workplaces to adapt to changing circumstances and operate in a culture that supports experimentation without blame. This attitude has undoubtedly contributed to the company's impressive growth.

How do we know this? We know it because Lush have made it a mainstay of their operation, have stated it publicly and thereafter stood by it. Fear can lead to the avoidance of risk, and allowing staff the chance to learn quickly and move on from any mistakes, makes potential risks more manageable. This in turn has led to a faster rate of innovation and improvement, and it is something that could apply to any team, no matter how small.

The great thing about these standards is that they extend to all of the company's practises — even the marketing. Lush, in fact, does not spend money on television campaigns, or celebrity and social media endorsements, and relies instead on user-generated content. It works brilliantly. The company even allows its staff the freedom to engage in 'random acts of kindness' where they are allowed to give away products to customers for a variety of positive reasons.

For Lush, the consideration of a staff's wellbeing is a value at the forefront of its mission statement, and the company has profited as a result. Openness also figures high in their value system. Visiting Lush shops — experiencing the brand firsthand — and speaking to their staff, it is easy for customers to feel this openness. Just as there are no secrets regarding their products, there appear to be no company secrets from the staff, any 'closed-room' meetings, and an overall transparency and lack of blame in dealing with issues.

In carrying these values off the webpage and across the company, we wanted to explore how these values work in practise, and across such a large company with so many outlets across the world. How do Lush go about creating their welcoming, relaxed atmosphere? Did they seek feedback from their staff on their workplace experience?

Nikki Williams is People Experience Manager at Lush. Her email signature has the words 'Putting People First' at the foot. Those few words tell us we're dealing with a considered corporate culture. She says:

"We train all our staff to be welcoming and open to

> all customers, with a fun and relaxed atmosphere. This happens naturally with our staff and customers. Every staff member actively contributes to the culture of the workplace. The staff tend to give feedback on their workplace to their managers directly. We do a yearly engagement survey with Ethical Consumer called Lush Listens, asking staff for their feedback. Our directors, senior managers and all shop and factory managers are very approachable for our employees."

That openness is witnessed in every healthy workplace and it makes mistreatment much less of a possibility. At Lush, we can see how this receptiveness breaks down potential barriers and fosters more positive working relationships.

> "Staff are encouraged to be curious and ask questions. Our co-founder Mark Constantine is very approachable — he's on Facebook and people do contact him. He encourages people to get involved," Nikki continues.

It should be true of every workplace that if an employee has a problem then they can go to their manager, and in larger organisations it helps if everyone can also thereby see the managers being managed.

Lush have made a significant investment in their managers and trust them to treat employees with respect.

> "If an employee ever comes to the People Experience team then the People Experience team will always ask first: "Have you spoken to your manager?" If the issue is serious and can't be resolved, then it will be referred to the retailer and at that point the team would consider a mediated meeting," says Nikki. "Our managers across the business are empowered and given autonomy to run the shops as if it was their own business. We trust that our managers are providing their employees with a great experience. We also look at our annual survey which, while a snapshot, provides a useful picture. We are looking to more frequent pulse checks and ways to open more two-way communication to our staff. Our People Experience and Retail team are available to managers and staff should tensions arise."

Growth is another word which features for Lush — not the adding zeros kind — the people growth kind. Says Nikki: "We believe in growth and people growing with us. Developing their skills. They do that best if their workplace is positive. Trust is a big issue too. People are properly empowered to carry out their roles."

In ensuring company values are universally applied equally to all, Lush have cemented positive internal working relations. They have also demonstrated that when everybody knows what you stand for, including staff, management and customers, the public will get the message that they are a good place to shop. Why? Because their values values gel with those of their customers. The customers get the company — and the company gets them.

It's not just that no animals were harmed in the preparation of Lush's products. Lush have created an international business in which a few core values have meant that both the public and their own staff trust them implicitly. This is achieved through an openness and transparency among the management and the business owners — a statement of that openness — and an ability to monitor those values on a regular basis through dialogue and exchange with staff at all levels.

Lush doesn't have a strict disciplinary regime and instead looks at ways it can support their employees. They believe in what Nikki Williams describes as a 'ripple effect' — a good working environment which leads to a good customer experience. Lush checks in with their employees, and staff are encouraged to be 'vocal'. If something needs to be said, staff are encouraged to say it and not bottle it up. This is an antidote to the 'be quiet' and 'know your place' culture, and it has not happened by accident. What we see at Lush is that in being active in trying to get the best for and out of employees, a range of successful outcomes can be achieved. This has been a deliberate policy on the part of the company — making a fulfilling work experience centre-stage. Says Nikki Williams:

> "Good businesses are doing what we do — there are still a lot of dinosaurs around though. They need to get on board with putting people at the heart of business. They will need to go there to survive. A lot of this change is driven by millennials who are looking at work in a different way."

Millennials. That word again. So often saddled with negative baggage and sometimes with that word 'snowflake' in toe. However, for all that baggage, millennials really look like being at the forefront of shaping and civilising the workplace. Ruchika Tulshyan noted the same thing in an article from Forbes in February 2013 titled 'Millennials Have the Power to Banish Workplace Bullying' observing:

> "Millennials have grown up with anti-bullying campaigns in school. Having more information on what constitutes bullying makes them more vocal against it and less likely to put up with it."

The article references work from Dr Gary Namie, who identifies the internet as having a positive impact on workplace bullying. "Online forums dedicated to sharing stories have generally been supportive. 72% of people surveyed had never heard of workplace bullying before reading the term online," he observes. Sharing, you see, is caring.

Lush as a distinctly 'new breed' company might in part have established itself as one of best places to work by expressly listening to Millennials — those who reached adulthood around the turn of the 21st Century — and simply won't wear bullying in any of its forms. This group are now probably the most work savvy of all demographics and are slowly watching their values embed in the workplace. Marginalised by many, but not Lush. Lush listened and everybody — staff, managers, owners and customers — benefitted as a result.

ACAS — MANAGING SITUATIONS

ACAS — the Advisory, Conciliation and Arbitration Service — is a public body which covers Great Britain and aims to enhance working life by means of improved employment relations practice. ACAS is independent and impartial and does not side with anybody during disputes, but instead aims to help parties reach equable resolutions. ACAS are a valuable resource for workers, managers and company owners who seek to know more about the correct procedures in managing suspected, active and historic cases of workplace harassment and bullying. ACAS has a role in prevention also, and in 2018 developed a presentation called 'Behaviours at Work - Understanding the Unacceptable', showing the main routes open to companies and managers when dealing with bullying and harassment allegations. While the presentation is not in-depth training in dealing with workplace bullying, it does deal with the various processes which come up when an allegation of bullying or harassment is raised.

ACAS also offer an accreditation in workplace mediation. This is known as their CIWM — a Certificate in

Internal Workplace Mediation. This involves five days of training which equips and accredits people as mediators in their workplace. This is analogous to having a first aider in your place of work, and anyone who has seen workplace bullying behaviours close up will immediately see the benefits of training such a person.

To work in the capacity they do, ACAS remain clear about what is and what is not bullying. ACAS' working definition is developed from The Harassment Act, where bullying is specifically described as follows:

> 'Unwanted conduct related to a relevant protected characteristic, which has the purpose or effect of violating an individual's dignity or creating an intimidating, hostile, degrading, humiliating or offensive environment for that individual.'

The use of the Harassment Act is practical, but in reality it can't legislate against bullying behaviour, which may often include some common 'grey-area' type of conducts, which all of us will have seen at some point, and probably experienced. Harassment specifically includes the use of provocative language; the use of a patronising manner; innuendo; mockery; unwanted comments on dress / appearance; assault and sexual assault; displays of explicit material; and denigration of religion or belief — all of which are commonly observable and usually relate to a protected characteristic. Victimisation is even more specifically defined as when '… somebody is treated badly because they have made a complaint or raised a grievance under the Equality Act.'

The three routes forward in dealing with an accusation of mistreatment at work, as listed in the ACAS presentation Behaviours at Work - Understanding the Unacceptable are:

- Investigation
- Constructive Conversation
- and Mediation

What ACAS bring to the table in this conversation is neutrality. The working conditions of this neutrality dictate that it is for each individual to determine what behaviour is acceptable to them and what they find offensive.

In the same way, any company should be able to state in its policies what that company finds offensive and unacceptable — and in establishing who decides whether behaviour can be classed as bullying or not, we find one particular stand-out idea: the key factor is the effect on the individual and not the intention of the individual accused of the bullying behaviour.

This is because bullying behaviour is often observable by its results. Whether someone intended or did not intend to carry out bullying behaviour is not relevant. What is relevant is their behaviour, and the effect it has had on others. This is the single hardest thing to explain to individuals who have bullied.

The ACAS presentation 'Behaviours at Work - Understanding the Unacceptable' also highlights what ACAS call 'Constructive Conversations'. Such conversations are a preferred option to formal actions and should have to precede formal action in less serious cases.

This suggests that if it is possible, allegations can be approached informally at first, if an accuser and alleged harasser is happy with this. The aim of such conversations will always be to stop unwanted or negative behaviour quickly and with a minimum of fuss. Such conversations don't rule out formal action if the conversation doesn't go well, or if such action seems more appropriate after discussion. But very often huge savings in health and time can be made when managers are able to deal with matters informally and in this manner.

In addition, Constructive Conversations also rely on both parties being able to get in front of a manager, or whichever person has responsibility over the person committing the alleged behaviour. As an accuser in such a situation you should prepare ahead, follow a structure and know your objective.

ACAS reminds all parties that 'It's the evidence that counts, not your opinion'.

In light of this ACAS therefore asks managers and other mediators to note a person's refusal to answer questions; inconsistences in their responses; a refusal to be interviewed; discrepancies between policies and practices; and to be wary of statements from anonymous witnesses.

All of these responses might be considered to be warning signs insofar as they express points of view, or attitudes. They are all actions suggestive of a non-co-operative witness, and so undermine any process of adjudication.

Ron Inwood, Senior Advisor at ACAS, shared what he considered to be one of the most difficult cases of workplace bullying he'd encountered:

> "I dealt with a case where a manager was side-lined by a more senior manager. He was isolated and was not able to carry out his day to day duties as his authority was removed. There was no discussion about performance and there was not a suggestion of performance issues. The more senior manager wanted to operate a different model and also to restructure, but there was no money to do this. He therefore effectively created a new structure using the people he wanted and side-lined a few others. This manager did not recognise this as bullying behaviour. The more junior manager went absent with stress and eventually selected himself to leave the organisation — but this was after more than 12 months."

As an example of the complexity of workplace bullying, this story stands out. It may appear nuanced but it does define the bullying behaviour it describes by the outcome — the effect on the individual, and not the intention of the individual accused of the bullying behaviour.

In the UK, ACAS can visit your organisation and help you understand what needs to be done to address a range of issues, and then work with you to develop practical solutions.

This can include resolving disputes with mediation, but preventative measures are just as important, and ACAS will help companies tackle bullying and harassment, work with them to develop policies, and more. As talking about bullying is one way that we suppress it, this clarifying approach is to everybody's benefit — especially if as a company or workgroup we don't know how to deal with it.

ACAS also has a free e-learning course on bullying and

harassment which you can register for at acas.org.uk/elearning and there you can also access a range of other ACAS e-learning topics.

Finally, there is the option with ACAS to train your own internal workplace mediator — the Certificate in Workplace Mediation.

This is a great idea.

Sometimes there arise points of no return between staff. Having a trained mediator on hand means that someone can get in quickly, talk things through and calm a situation down.

If fights and other tense situations arise, as they sometimes do, a person with a CIWM will save time, money and productivity by being a recognised point of contact and a safe pair of hands.

Such solutions have lasting results and are more positive than Employment Tribunals which are expensive, time-consuming and stressful. Company owners — no matter how small the business — could think of such a person in the same light as they might a first aider.

For larger companies, there is no excuse at all not to train such a person from among your staff.

Armed with an accredited certification from ACAS' five-day course, as well as a working knowledge of their company's values, a business's internal mediator will work wonders in bringing the costs of workplace bullying and harassment nearer to naught than any other person there.

VALUES IN PRACTISE

In building ANTI-BULLY, INC. — our ground zero business template designed to eliminate bullying behaviours from the workplace — we need to think of ways that we can live up to our stated values, and ways in which we can also demonstrate that we have lived up to them.

Most importantly, our values can't just languish on a whiteboard or on the company website. The danger is they will be ignored. The values need to be part of the company's roadmap and built into its DNA. This is how values will help get any company to where it seeks to be.

We say this, because these values need to be alive. By being alive and a part of the team, values can offer a shared and guiding authority that is not just safe, but is a higher principle which all can turn to.

It means that the greatest authority in the company isn't that czar-like boss who believes they are right and consequently has no patience for those who disagree. That is the high road to bullying. It means that when someone misbehaves with suggestive touching or language, a temper tantrum, or any other form of emotional abuse, the arbiter isn't going to be the loudest most powerful individual in the room, but instead is going to be a living abstract in the form of a value.

This is why, although it may seem strange to a society that doesn't always believe in gods, ghosts or magic of any kind, that we are still wise to think of these values as alive.

This is easy to put into practice and if it helps, then the values can be embodied in a token of some sort, something that everybody can see as a reminder. This is why the ancients kept statues of their gods at hand and revered them. The statues were a constant reminder of the values to which they aspired.

It is also the origin of ritual prayer. Such prayers, because they were a physical action, served to reinforce the values and reminded those who spoke them that they didn't live in a chaotic and out of control universe, where they were going to be at the mercy of anyone stronger and more bullying than they were. When I repeat my values to myself before I go to work or before I go into an important meeting, I am doing something not dissimilar. In repeating those values, I am not only reminding myself of my most important tools, I am also ensuring that my chances of success are higher. I am reminding myself that when problems arise, I have something to turn to. If there is a problem, or if someone has messed up or upset me, because I can recall my values I don't need to resort to bullying or any other bad behaviour.

Every company, large or small, will benefit from this discussion of values. The size of the company doesn't matter, either. The Cyrenians, as discussed in an earlier chapter, has about 150 staff and one of them is employed to, among other things, monitor the company's values. Regular meetings with all staff are a part of this process and help to develop ways in which these values can be implemented and acted upon. This single person investment unarguably represents money well spent. The Cyrenians looks and feels like a happy workplace, where nobody feels pressured or upset — and if they do, there are frameworks in place to address anything.

On a lesser scale and even in a small company or team of any sort, the same is achievable. All that is required are the values themselves — and one staff member or business-owner appointed to make sure that the company's values inform daily routine, as well as short and long-term goals. It means that if we do not like the values of the company we work for, we can either go to another company, or petition our current company to change their values. This works so long as everybody knows the values and is aware that nobody is exempt from them.

There is a mindset which will view this as nonsense — a mindset which takes the tunnel-visioned and dictatorial 'my way or the highway' approach to the work experience. By all means go and work for these people, but be careful — they are likely to be bullies. Anyone who ridicules the idea of a workplace being 'value-led' is going to be a potential danger to your health and well-being. An individual who belittles an initiative such as establishing and agreeing 'company values' will just want you to do things their way, and potentially even punish you if you don't comply. Any manager or owner who will not publicly state their company's values believes in some way that they don't need to, because it is 'their' company or 'their' team. They are likely not a good person to work with and may believe that because you work for them, they also own your labour and the right to abuse it, and maybe even you with it. Beware.

The benefits aren't just human. Companies save significant amounts in terms of money, inefficiency and blocked decision-making and create a more efficient company, a more pleasant working environment and improved group mental health — when they are led by values.

Everything listed below can be put in place by any company, small or large if it genuinely seeks to be a safe place to work:

1. At ANTI-BULLY, INC. the company values are clear from the first point of contact — they will be included in the job listing. The same values will also be found across every job description at ANTI-BULLY, INC. and also be on the application form for every role at the company. Expect these values to be a part of the job interview too! You can't be expected to work at this company if you don't know the company values, or if you are not willing to adopt them.

2. At ANTI-BULLY, INC. support tools are offered to the staff. These could include counselling, bike-to-work schemes, childcare vouchers, self-care and well-being workshops, mentoring and staff lunches. There is no end to the amount of support tools a company can offer, and there is no excuse for small companies who may argue that they cannot afford these ideas.

Can they afford not to? What is important about such support tools is consistent across all sizes of company however: the support tools must be available at all times and are never mandatory. Maybe a staff member will need one or all of the company's support tools at any given time — or maybe they never will. What is important is that the support tools are available to all, and known to be available.

3. At ANTI-BULLY, INC. staff have the opportunity to ask questions about the company's values. The company recognises this by creating such opportunities, as in one-to-one meetings and other regular engagements. Team meetings, or support and supervisory meetings are a place for reflection on the company's values. Once again, this needs to happen. If it does not, the values with gather dust, and staff will be at risk from disruptive practices.

4. At ANTI-BULLY, INC. you may be asked about your own values. This isn't just an exercise for management, but as the staff flourish, so will the company. Staff are encouraged to take the lead by understanding their own aims and values. The sort of things that stop this happening are blame culture and an environment where people become scared of making mistakes. Asking staff about their own values also encourages people to find their voice, and to realise where that voice can be heard. Most of us don't know what our values are, so this is a great opportunity to find out what they might be.

5. At ANTI-BULLY, INC. the managers find ways to measure how successfully the company's values have been applied. All firms that state what their values are should of course also devise ways in which these can be measured. Staff questionnaires are a good way to do this, but it doesn't end there. The Fair Work Convention Scotland (2016) is one of the best documents about how this kind of thing can be achieved. It covers a multitude of positive factors, focusing on the values of Security, Respect, Effective Voice, Opportunity and Fulfilment. It is a manager's job to monitor these things, and if you don't feel you have access to any of these five values, it's worth asking why. You may be working at BULLY, INC.

6. At ANTI-BULLY, INC. we allow staff to take an interest in other jobs and departments in the same company. This doesn't just foster a greater involvement, but it dispels secrecy and pigeon-holing. Never be told that something is none of your business. Never be told that your own work is nobody else's business. Transparency is everything and it helps for example to prepare an annual skills audit, which lists your own skills and responsibilities. Your work should be transparent, as should that of the management. Secret meetings are an absolute no-go and it helps enormously if, as a part of your job, you have a written record of your contacts, preferred methods of work and what you do from day to day. This benefits you, the company and those that do your job after you have moved on.

These are a handful of tools that are available which could make the difference between safety at work, and a bully's paradise. At the time of writing, The Cyrenians charity has no less than 86 such tools in place! Implementing these tools has ensured that the company has remained true to its values, and in doing so it has achieved success not just in its stated mission, but also in staff well-being. The two are, of course, inextricably linked and this company has been operating with continued reference to the same set of values for over 50 years now — a huge achievement.

Now, cast your mind back to BULLY, INC. and ask what the workplace bully would make of all that? The agreed and shared values? The regular monitoring and checking-in? The assigned staff dedicated to maintaining these values and everybody feeling free and empowered to flag up problems if things go wrong? The access to support tools? The liberty to ask questions?

Much of this will depend on the company culture and the company culture will very likely depend on the people in charge.

Writer and entrepreneur Ted Coiné has made a point of studying this chain of unfortunate events, and explains how this happens. It's almost as if such bullying cultures are too big to observe:

> "The top leader of a company — the founder or CEO — determines the culture, and is its key defender. Granted, many leaders have no clue about culture, so their company culture is weak and inconsistent. But when you see a healthy culture in a thriving company, that is inevitably the result of very

> intentional culture building from the very top. I cannot name a single case of an owner or CEO changing an existing culture deep into their tenure. Culture change, when it happens, is most often pulled off with a fresh leader. The good news for large companies is, CEO turnover is close to once every three years. Okay, that's actually really disruptive and is a sign of a systemic disease that needs radical addressing. But it's good in that every three years or so, there's a fresh set of eyes in the C-suite and an energy to make change if they have the will and know how."

And what is that know-how exactly?

> "What I've noticed in my work as a customer experience researcher, is that only the top companies, maybe the healthiest and best-led ten percent or less, have any idea what this enlightened self-interest means in theory, and even fewer have the requisite skills to pull it off. If you want my one bottom line for any worker looking for a healthier work environment, it's this: find an employer that is already excellent. Change only comes to companies that want to change, and that starts with the number one person in charge. Any leader who has been in place for more than a short while who suddenly sees the light? You aren't being overly cynical to be wary of a transformation like that."

This is why values may be something that everyone can get

behind, as something that can be quickly and effectively instituted. Any person prone to bullying behaviour will be hostile to this — so watch out for them. We cannot make a bullying individual or anyone else adhere to our shared thinking if they choose not to do so, but we can protect ourselves, our health and our company's profits by ring-fencing them with values.

If your company or workgroup does not have a stated set of values, you can also take the lead by requesting that one-to-one or team meetings be held at which these values are discussed.

Remember that if a person refuses to discuss these matters at work, this is a sure sign of trouble. The likelihood of this person being a bully is, regrettably, high.

THE END OF THE STORY?

BULLYING AS A CAREER KILLER

Bullying isn't just about what happens in the here and now. It is also a potential career wrecker. Sustained bullying has the capacity to force individuals to change the way they earn a living, where they do it, and for whom. When we start to discuss bullying behaviours at work, it turns out there are many more people among us than we realised, who have had to leave their jobs because of it.

In some cases that can mean having to embark on not just a new job, but a whole new career, maybe even junking years of training and experience in the painful process.

Statistically, it's unlikely that our first encounter with bullying will be at work. Our formative years, specifically those spent at school, define our outlook on life as adults and it's at school that a lot of us witness what bullying looks like and feels like.

In a survey commissioned by Oxford Open Learning Trust and carried out by YouGov in 2014 more than half of UK adults said they were bullied at school on at least one occasion with 65% of those surveyed saying it had damaged their self-confidence. On top of this, 36% believed it had a negative effect on their ability to make friends and 27% stated that it had adversely affected their mental health. These experiences are, however reluctantly, dragged with us into adult life and impact what we do, who we end up being and how we interact with others.

Commenting on the effect of childhood bullying into adulthood, Ian Rivers, formerly professor of Human Development at Brunel University London, and now Professor of Education for Social Change at Strathclyde University said (telegraph.co.uk, 07.08.2014):

> "Previous research has shown that people who have been bullied have difficulty forming and maintaining lasting intimate relationships. In terms of their future prospects, you also see that children who have been bullied try and get out of school as early as possible. This often means that they don't stay on until sixth form and do A-levels. Thus, they don't have the qualifications for the types of jobs that they might be suited for."

Louise Arseneault, Professor at the Institute of Psychiatry at King's College London, agrees that the correlation between classroom and playground experiences where bullying has been prevalent, and later life, is obvious and significant:

> "People who have been bullied in childhood are less likely to do well in terms of employment and salary, and they seem to achieve a little bit less in terms of their education as well."

She adds:

> "If you are bullied at school you will be less motivated to learn there. What is surprising though was that the effects (of bullying) are lasting up until midlife."

Indeed, the bullying fallout is still prevalent when we reach our 50s with higher incidences than average of depression, poor physical health and anxiety being reported.

Bullying is, from an early age, potentially smothering some of us. Or quite a lot of us. What this appears to amount to is that life possibilities are skewed simply because of our exposure to a playground menace. Our potential as human beings is compromised and undermined.

One of the most fertile environments for bullying in the United Kingdom is the NHS (National Health Service). In a Guardian survey dated October 2016, some 81% of respondents who worked within the NHS agreed that they had experienced bullying at work and a further 44% claimed that the bullying was an ongoing issue in their work lives. An astonishing 87% agreed that bullying was a big issue within the NHS.

In a most affecting account of her bullying within the NHS, an anonymous female shared her experience and despair (The Guardian, 14.04.2016), starting with her self-identification as a target. She wrote:

> "When a woman was hired to work in my department, it became clear that she was not all she seemed and her attitude to work and patient care became a case

> for concern. I soon found myself the target of her calculated actions."

The health implications for an individual dealing with relentless bullying emerged for her:

> "My mental health declined, and I was put on very high doses of antidepressants and felt such despair that my beloved career and life were slowly dying. I wanted to die — despite being a single mother at the time, I couldn't face life anymore. I was deskilled, devalued and isolated."

Her story ended after an 18-month battle during which she was the subject of an internal investigation, which seemed to her to be at best inept, and at worst uncaring.

Taking the decision to leave for this employee did not signify an ending — something that is common with all targets of bullying behaviour. Yes, she had exerted a level of control in choosing to resign. But the sense of loss for her is still vivid when she speaks of "her beloved NHS". And her own sense of trauma:

> "I will never forget what happened to me, and four years on I still suffer trauma whenever I go near the hospital where I once worked. No action was taken against my bully even though it was acknowledged that she had an attitude problem, and this was not the first time they had had complaints against her. I will never be able to work in the NHS again because I have seen a side that I never thought existed."

Even charities — where it might be reasonable to assume a higher level of workplace integrity and stability might exist — are not immune. Revelations in a report into the inner workings at Amnesty International (February 2019) had one worker quoted as saying:

> "There was a real culture of bullying, right up until I left [several years ago] particularly of middle managers. It was well known the management team were kept very much in line, and anyone who stepped out of line was very publicly humiliated."

The tropes of belittling and threatening play here as well. In the private sector things are the same. David, 40s, who works in media recalled his experience of systemic and sustained bullying and undermining, but with a twist. He didn't initially see it:

> "I was fortunate enough to occupy a senior position within the company I worked at; I was 'creative' and generated profitable ideas and products. However, it took a while to recognise I was no less immune to slights and put downs. I made the calculation monetarily and it was just about worth it to carry on. I did over a decade there. But the cost really only kicked in after I left. I realised the strain and pressures I'd worked under — including pretty much 24/7 contactability — had resulted in total burnout. I took easily a couple of years to repair."

That whole issue of tolerance and what we're prepared to

endure to sustain a job, underpins bullying. And many of us are reduced to calculating it in cold hard cash. Examples of behaviours that could over time persuade an individual to consider their position — and their capacity to endure their day-to-day — would include:

- **Contract manipulation**: where someone is pushed into accepting a lower salary, or poorer conditions of work, reduced holidays and benefits.

- **Repeated belittling**: where individuals are humiliated in front of co-workers, with their work and attitude and 'fit' being called into question.

- **Isolating / Undermining**: this involves starving an individual of knowledge and information they require to function properly within the work context, and then attacking them for underperforming. This doesn't necessarily include overt anger or similar abuse but might be something like constantly questioning the individual over why they chose action 'A' over 'B' and injecting self-doubt into their work experience.

Life after leaving a job because of bullying is not an easy place. One recruitment consultant I spoke to, who opted to remain anonymous, said:

> "The trouble is, no employer really wants to hear that a potential new employee has been bullied. Quite simply, it's a turn off. It triggers all sorts of negative thoughts in them about the candidate. Could they be

trouble? Or even what's wrong with them? That's why I never advise clients to use the word 'bullied' in an interview for those reasons."

This is the last thing a bullying individual at work considers. Once the target is out of the door, other processes begin. For the bullying individual, the scapegoating will probably be ramped up as the target won't be there to defend themselves. For the target (and their family) there is unemployment, life rebuilding, ill-health and other difficulties. For the bystanders there is an abiding sense of doubt, which managers and business owners should be aware, is not conducive to productivity.

Finally, there is often a feeling among survivors who have been bullied out of a job that they will never recover from the experience.

It is admittedly, a negative idea. But we must never forget that workplace bullying is emotional abuse, just as much as it is a personal assault, and it represents behaviours and events that never needed to happen and never should have happened.

Just as we respect the voices of the targets of physical and sexual assault, we likewise understand that once a person has been bullied out of a job, their life has been altered by factors beyond their control.

Bullying is something that does not need to happen and is by definition the wrong answer to a situation. If someone is creating difficulties for you at work, bullying is not the answer to the situation — which is why a set of values can protect not just targets — but can protect us all from resorting to such behaviours.

The post-bullying landscape is a little-known place given that most therapeutic and human resources energy tends to focus on active bullying situations. For teachers and health professionals in particular, who have trained specifically for one vocation, this is an empty, lonely and in exceptional cases, a suicidal place. As recently as March 2018 a 30-year-old female nurse at a hospital in Swansea committed suicide. A five-month investigation into her death concluded the cause to be sustained bullying, with the authors of the resulting report describing her working conditions as 'difficult' and detailing how she was regularly sworn at and given the worst shifts at the hospital.

People who witness bullying at work, similarly, don't get the chance to see what happens to the person who has left. If bystanders who see someone being bullied out of a job think that the target is just going to start working in the same capacity in another workplace the following week, they are doing more than turning a blind eye. They are contributing to the bullying behaviour, and the bullies are probably relying on this.

This is why nobody really knows about this post-bullying place unless they have been there. It's an unproductive place, where personal development is stalled, or maybe even regressing, and it is a place of scars and fear, and people can end up wandering there, alone and unwell, for a long time.

Self-confidence is always a casualty in any instance of workplace bullying and rebuilding it is not an overnight process.

These are the realities of bullying as a career killer. Where individuals have their lives upended, their career trajectories interrupted, their freedom to progress and prosper in the workplace extinguished. Where betterment is blocked. Where professional work vocation can be wrenched from them permanently and work and indeed life opportunities are snuffed out.

Did we overstate how life-altering bullying can be, do you think? No, neither do we.

THE BULLY PREMIUM

Tolerance for bullying and sexual impropriety in the workplace has changed. Behaviours that were once considered to be inevitable can now be examined in light of shared values and workplaces can become safer and happier environments. We've already discussed companies that have suffered because of the bullying behaviours of managers and owners, and even seen companies that have closed for these reasons. It follows that as well as improvements in worker well-being, the eradication of bullying behaviour can lead to improved productivity. This got us thinking about whether or not anyone could put a figure on that. There will certainly be managers and company owners out there that will respond positively to this knowledge — because even if they don't care about worker well-being — they are very likely to care about their bottom line.

Bullying behaviour certainly has a price. It costs, and if businesses don't consider this, they are overlooking issues around productivity, as well as risking health and safety. The two are so thoroughly linked that there is no excuse. Happiness is productivity — and the converse is expensive. When acceptable behaviours are exceeded — be it via bullying, sexual harassment, or embedded bigotry towards minorities — and individuals either get paid off or bailed out by their employer — we often consider this to be a satisfactory result. It's all about making awkward things go away.

Google is a good place to start for a globalised case study. This is a company that inhabits the upper echelons of pretty much every Best Place To Work guide under the sun — a business ranked number one Best Company To Work For by Fortune magazine — a spot it has occupied for the last six years.

The company pays top dollar; your working environment is cutting edge; you eat free. There are doctors on site. You can bring your pet in if you want. They even offer 'massage credits' — a reward for good work where you can lie on your front and be pummelled into a better posture. Google is with you during major life events, like pregnancy. They aren't stingy about maternity leave. They do buy into the whole 'happy worker is a better worker' thing.'

But at Google you can also receive a massive pay-out for being implicated in sexual misconduct — if you are the right man in the right position. The company recently shelled out some $135m in exit packages to two executives who were accused of precisely that. And it sickened employees so much that around 20,000 Google staffers went on strike at the tail end of 2018.

This strike was nobody's outdated stereotype of clichéd worker-versus-boss showdown in a Marxist paradigm. It wasn't about trying to leverage more pay or shorter hours. It was about company values and how many workers felt these values had been trampled upon and abused.

The worker moral disquiet at Google — which inspired a global walk out across Google's whole empire — bled significantly into the #MeToo movement, which was centre stage at that point. It was decidedly awkward for Google. The strikers' message to Google was clear and unequivocal: they were unhappy with a company culture that to their knowledge was effectively covering up and smothering instances of harassment.

In doing so the workers leveraged the prestige of working at Google to generate a news story which circulated around the world — ranking on Google's flagship search engine in the process — and gave Google Corporate a bloody nose. The company's Chief Executive Officer Sundar Pichar did what he needed to do and discreetly aligned himself with the demonstrators by sending an email in which he acknowledged the issue of harassment 'had persisted for far too long in our society' (clever and slightly deflecting) and offered protestors 'the support you need'. The Google Walkout For Real Change has not disbanded and still has a social media account on Twitter: @GoogleWalkout).

The culture the protestors were complaining about enabled senior executives with credible accusations against them to leave Google with massive severance pay-outs in the process, and crystallised in the case of the 'Father of Android' — Andy Rubin — who left Google with a payment of $90m dollars — one of the most conspicuous examples of corporate trousering in history.

While Google's CEO Larry Page issued a public statement wishing 'Andy all the best with what's next' an accusation of sexual misconduct emerged into the public domain. Rubin was accused of sexual coercion by the woman with whom he was having an extra marital relationship. The accusation was investigated by Google and ultimately led to a request for Rubin's resignation. But the unpalatable truth remained: the $90m severance worked out at $2m per month for four years — an amount that was entirely discretionary. Contractually Google could have paid a fraction of that.

In January of 2019 shareholders filed a lawsuit against Google's parent company Alphabet over pay-outs made to executives accused of sexual harassment and called for executives who received pay-outs to return them. One of the lawyers filing the suits, Louise Renne, commented:

> "There has been substantial evidence of sexual harassment at Google. And yet there hasn't been the appropriate follow-through. In fact, quite to the contrary. The perpetrators of the sexual harassment have been rewarded handsomely — in one case, by a $90m pay-out. And that's just wrong."

There was also the inference that Larry Page and Google paid up to ensure Rubin's silence. According to theverge.com (20.01.2019), Google feared that 'if they fired Rubin for cause, he would sue Google for wrongful termination and all the tawdry details of sexual harassment by senior executives (at Google) would become public.'

And that's Google. One of the best workplaces on the planet. Illustrating how buying one's way out of trouble at the most senior corporate level — is a thing. It's the price of business and a genuine 'bully premium'.

Next let's look at the biggest employer in the UK — and the fifth biggest single employer in the world — the NHS. According to a study published in the journal Public Money & Management — that figure is £2bn per year in England alone while bullying in isolation could be identified as costing upwards of £600m resulting in anxious employees making more errors, while a further £300m was identified as sickness attributed to bullying. A quarter of NHS England staff claim to have suffered from bullying by colleagues.

The issue also infects Higher Education in the UK with £90m being paid out by universities from 96 education establishments between 2017 and 2019 with the cases involved numbering over 4,000.

The financial implications of these bully premiums are hard to piece together with the catch-all prevalence of non-disclosure agreements. A 2018 survey for the Prospect Union in the UK found that 35% of women had suffered sexual harassment at work. As the old cliché goes, do the math.

One senior board member of a FTSE Top 100 company corroborated that 'pay to play' payments were a reality in the UK private sector:

> "At senior level, there's an awful lot of testosterone. Aggression. And money. Many of these guys are used to getting what they want whether it's a Lamborghini

> or a flat. They're not used to hearing 'no' in any context. Things happen. And when they do, they have to be hushed up for what is perceived as the good of the company. That's what matters to directors and shareholders."

And the answer is money?

> "What other answer would there be? If you need to get rid of a difficult situation, that's what you use."

Did he think it was possible to put a figure on that in terms of turnover for an average company — this fiscal corrective to make difficult things go away?

> "If average means little companies then I don't know; but big companies easily are looking at 4% and more."

This is the world we live in.

It's pay-to-play at its most basic. It's managing collateral damage as corporate policy. And we call it the Bully Premium.

These are of course the large scale cases, and yet every single business must have such a premium, somehow hidden until such time as the proverbial hits the fan and the costs begin to mount. It's become apparent that bullying is expensive, and that as a health and safety issue it is going to cost every business in many different ways. Certainly, the reasons we tackle bullying at work are human, and our emphasis is upon worker well-being. But there is another factor here, and that is cost. Even if we were to live in a world in which bullies reigned supreme, those same bullying individuals would still have to face up to the fact that if they want a more productive company or department, then the way to achieve it is by means of sound company values — and an emphasis on eradicating bullying behaviours.

If you'd like to know what your own company or workgroup's Bully Premium is, then we've got an online calculator that will put a value on that for you. The Bully Premium calculator is free to download, and requires some basic figures such as company turnover, and staff days lost to mental health each year. The Bully Premium calculator was developed by experts in workplace bullying, after consultation with an accountancy firm. The figure that it will give you will be a close approximation to just how much money your own firm is losing to workplace bullying each and every year.

To access the calculator, visit **bully-inc.com**.

NO APOLOGIES

It was one of the craziest feelings of my life. I'd turned up for work on Monday morning but by midday I'd left the premises for good. There were no goodbyes, and no farewell drinks with my colleagues, because I think my colleagues were unsure of what to say or how to act.

What started as a regular Monday morning one-to-one, turned into an ambush meeting. With no warning I was told that I was bad at my job and then a list appeared which amounted to 13 months of grievances against me. None of this was mentioned in any kind or constructive way, and some of it was even shouted at me at close range. The meeting ended with my being told that all of our workgroup — over a dozen people — agreed that I was not fit for my job — and then the bullying person speaking to me stormed out. Nobody had ever spoken to me like that before and it was humiliating and frightening, and I could not go back to that place until it was acknowledged.

It is conceivable that this bullying individual had real grievances against me, but of course they blew their chance to air this in any proper manner, instead revealing a pattern of up to 13 months of behind-the-scenes 'evidence gathering' followed by a burst of emotional abuse. This ambush event was never acknowledged and yet the consequences were widely felt. Certainly, I no longer had a job — but it changed the lives of others too. The secrecy and the feeling of fear which remained in that workplace after my surprise departure were contributing factors in that company's decline.

Bullying is always a health issue. All evidence informs us of this, but research on bullying in the workplace in the last decade has also shown the financial consequences for any affected company. The 2012 study for Helsinki University titled *Workplace Bullying and Subsequent Psychotropic Medication* flatly demonstrated the expensive link between bullying at work and prescription medication among both bystanders and targets — in case there was any doubt. At the same time, researchers at the University of Manitoba in Winnipeg presented 21 years' worth of findings showing the health impact of bullying, indicating that while there are nearly always systems in place for dealing with sexual harassment at work, the medical and financial impact of bullying is far worse because of the exact opposite — a lack of preparation.

Sandy Hershcovis, who was one of the team conducting the University of Manitoba study said:

> "Workplace bullying doesn't have any policy attention, there's no legal recourse you can take, so really you're stuck and there's no coping mechanisms that you can try to use to overcome the situation."

Workplace bullying in all its guises persists for the lack of these policies. It persists because so few workplaces care to define the specific behaviours involved, and it persists because bullying individuals often get their way.

One common policy seems to be to be to encourage staff to 'put their foot down' regarding bullying, as they do in schools. Company policies and government policies can't always be clear about bullying, because they can't automatically legislate for all specific behaviours and personal values. There can however be a connection between behaviour and values which can be observed by all, and understood enough to be discussed without anyone having to resort to emotionally abusive modes of communication.

The bullying behaviour I experienced followed me out of the door in the form of emails and other messages, and there was also a period of scapegoating. For months after that, failings at that workplace could be attributed to me — "that was Peter's fault."

I don't believe that anyone can appreciate such emotional damage until they have experienced it. Certainly, the bullying individual I encountered gave it no thought. That person went to work the next day along with everyone else and told me later in an email that things were much better at the workplace without me. This illustrated once more what I believe is the single most fearsome aspect of any bullying behaviour — the outcome.

Sometimes all we have is the outcome. Sometimes targets don't see the bullying behaviour coming, or if they do they fail to act because their confidence is already damaged or because there is no 'proof'. When all we are left with is the outcome then we need to piece things together from there. This is far from satisfactory, because it follows that much of what we learn about bullying behaviour is discovered in retrospect.

As it was, everyone went to work the next day as normal. I am sure there were whispers and doubts but I was not there to hear them — and yet I would have given a lot to have left that job as I left all of the other jobs I have had — with a handshake, a goodbye drink, and a smile from those whom I left behind.

Mary O'Neill, regards bullying as:

1. Prolonged and sustained behaviour which is
2. Detrimental to the health (mental or physical) of the target.

Mary continues:

> "The major trends I notice working with a lot of public sector employees, is the impact of austerity on the incidence of reported workplace hostility. Budgets are cut, and people must do more with less and so people feel stressed. As a result, polite behaviour is abandoned. It becomes adversarial and abrasive.
>
> "Furthermore, people are sometimes promoted above their skill level and have no experience of managing a team, there is no funding for staff training and so they are thrown in the deep end. They have no idea how to manage a team and so they resort to an autocratic management style.

> "Often targets of bullying will say that they experience the manager as 'out of their depth'. The most common phrase I hear from targets is that the manager will say: 'Well, you just have to get on with it…' which I interpret to mean that there is nothing I (the manager) can do about it — so just keep doing what you're doing even though it's not working and don't bother me. Research has shown worker engagement is crucial to a business success."

I have asked targets of bullying to hold on to their authority. By authority I mean that if you feel you have been the target of bullying you will be challenged about what happened to you. You will be challenged about what bullying is and whether it occurred. You absolutely must know the answers to all of these questions if you are going to get involved in reporting or resolving an incidence of bullying.

This is the meaning of authority. It refers to the authority you have over your story. Remember that bystanders, family and friends might be right if they tell you that what you have experienced is not bullying.

Bystanders meantime must allow a target to maintain authority over their story. #MeToo reminds us that being listened to and being believed are foundational to the relief of any upset and trauma. It is bullying behaviour to try and shut down these conversations and to dismiss the stories of targets. Mary O'Neill reminds us that one thing that bullies always do is 'deny the target's experience.' This happens every time with bullying, because it is the safest way for an abuser to escape responsibility.

Often bystanders don't define an incident as bullying. Yet, the higher a person is in the management structure, the more they must be aware of bullying behaviour and demonstrate that they know it when they see it — or do it. Sometimes, when targets complain to those above them in the hierarchy, the manager doesn't define the event as bullying and the target is seen as being a complainer, or as being too sensitive.

The very best thing that we can do to help ourselves become better bystanders, is to act on our organisational values.

This means that potential bystanders to bullying should receive some basic training in the following factors. All this training need involve is discussion. If this happens, then we may approach that ideal state in which we are all bystanders who are able to:

- Describe and recognise bullying behaviours based on stated company values;

- Understand that silence typically enforces bullying;

- Feel safe in providing information while also being comfortable that they are protecting themselves.

By and by, I would advocate that everyone should try editing that list to suit the needs of their own working environment.

If that is done, any person alleging something can hold on to their authority if bullying is a live issue. It is extremely tiring holding on to that kind of authority. The worry about being heard makes a person exceptionally tired, and it also makes the whole workplace tired if everyone is waiting for a situation to resolve and if it is not happening for lack of acknowledgement.

While we are speaking about waiting, I should add that waiting for a bully to apologise is the longest, hardest, coldest experience an injured party may have. It's like being in the bleakest bus shelter at the highest point on the loneliest Arctic ice road.

To avoid this wait, I would emphasise that bullies don't need to apologise. It's not the most important part of the process. It might sound strange and seem unnatural — but bullies do not need to apologise.

Here is how Acknowledgement and Restitution really work. For the emotional difficulties bullying has caused there is a straightforward way for that tension and pain to begin to be released — and it is an acknowledgement that what happened, really happened. This is not just good for the targeted person but it is good for everyone in the workplace because it allows business to return to its ordained pace.

An apology is not included and an apology is not needed. Good apologies are hard to do anyway, and you have to be quite wise or self-aware to either write or verbalise a true one. This is why it isn't wise to press a bullying individual into apologising. First of all, bullies don't tend to apologise, and a lack of the above qualities will probably mean that if they do, they will make a botch of it by issuing a false or loaded apology. I have seen an email 'apology' from someone who was found to be bullying another worker and in it the bully says that while they regretted their verbal abuses and intimidation of their colleague, they wanted to add that their abusive shouting only happened once with that particular person and that they were provoked! This short statement is packed not just with falsity, but with a bully's ignorance.

Bear in mind then, that apologies are not going to be the most important thing here. Acknowledgment is however non-negotiable, because without it that means there's no chance of Restitution.

That is why Acknowledgement is so important because it's the only way we can we reach a point of Restitution.

In Restitution we are restoring an ideal — we are restoring the place where we all wanted to work to begin with. It's important that the bully, the bystanders and the target of any bullying know that there is only one way to this place — and it is through a process of Acknowledgement.

Be warned — but after a targeted person leaves a workplace because of bullying, there is sometimes no Acknowledgment, because the person 'causing trouble' has gone. This is wrong for many reasons and it is not Restitution.

In cases which have involved significant loss of earnings and health, Restitution might cover recompense for injury or loss, or more properly the restoration of something lost or stolen, back to its proper owner.

Some will embark upon the former of these definitions, which points to a legal case of some kind, resulting in an official verdict and a possible award of damages. This is relatively rare compared to the amount of bullying that is reported, for the reasons that often highly specific circumstances need to be defined and demonstrated for there to be any legal case or hearing, and they need to be revisited over a long period of time, assessed and judged.

Restitution however, when it happens, is not solely for the targets of bullying — it is for everybody.

Restitution is for the entire workplace because what is being restored is the 'state of no bullying behaviour.'

Bullying will go unnoticed if bullying behaviours are not recognised or if they are named as something else. Claims of bullying made against the British Prime Minister (Gordon Brown) in 2010 (The Guardian 24.02.2010) were refuted with the message that the PM was 'not a bully', but that he was 'demanding, passionate and emotional.'

Clever words, which throw the emphasis back at those who felt targeted.

The fact is that across all working environments the circumstances of bullying behaviour are always the same. A bully will always argue that the target is the problem, when it is bullying behaviour that is first and finally the problem.

What is restored after an incident of bullying is up to everybody. And if a targeted person leaves, then the Restitution could mean continuing to condone bad behaviours. The choice is yours — it truly is!

You could verbalise it like this: "I am not going to assign responsibility to anyone else for what I am feeling."

This statement is apt, because making someone else responsible for your feelings and your problems is what gets us into bullying situations to begin with. If we've a struggle going on in our working life or elsewhere, we must consider looking for solutions within ourselves. Expecting someone else to change in order to sort out your own struggles is the first step to becoming a bully.

Targets of bullying who have been made into a

'problem' by someone else, understand this. These survivors have learned that every abusive thing that a bullying individual has said to them, written to them in emails and actioned against them, is the property of the bully and not their issue. This can be an exceptionally hard realisation to achieve, often because it is learned by being the subject of abusive behaviour.

But none of this is easy.

What is easy is bullying.

It's easy to shout and storm out and it's easy to blame someone else. It's even satisfying to divest yourself of responsibility and say: "It's all your fault!"

If you indulge in this, and can't find the answers to your situation within yourself — if you can't share values, goals and good manners with those you work with — then you might like to be the one that leaves the workplace and not the target.

Because you have just defined yourself as a bully.

ABOUT THE AUTHORS

Peter Burnett is a writer and publisher living in Scotland. He is the author of the following titles:

- The Machine Doctor (Thirsty Books, 2001)
- Odium (Argyll Publishing, 2004)
- The Supper Book (Leamington Books, 2008)
- The Studio Game (Fledgling Press, 2012)
- #freetopiary: An Occupy Romance (Thirsty Books, 2012; Skyhorse, 2013)
- Scotland or No (Capercaillie, 2014)
- How To Do Privacy in the 21st Century (Eyewear, 2018)
- French Toast (Thirsty Books, 2019)

facebook.com/leamingtonbooks
twitter.com/leamingtonbooks
instagram.com/leamingtonbooks

The issue of workplace bullying was central to work **Jonathan Richards** undertook for the NHS with mental health magazine ThereThere. As former Group Managing Editor at OK! Magazine with an insight into the machinations of celebrity, he writes extensively of bullying behaviours in the world of celeb/reality TV. In current role at financial channel LGBT Money he describes himself as being 'obsessive' about the well-being of all connected with the business. He views workplace bullying as the endemic social malaise of our times.

THE BULLY PREMIUM

How much is bullying costing your company? How much does it cost the economy? Visiting workplaces where bullying behaviour has been a problem, we've sometimes found that the best way to get through to company owners is by answering these very questions. Taking the view that prevention is better than cure, we've tried to explain to managers, owners and employees alike, that a system of shared values is going to help 'bully-proof' their working environment.

For those that don't see the benefits in this however, we've created the Bully Premium Calculator. This speaks to even the most abrasive and uncaring of company owners because it talks in a language they understand — the language of cost / benefit.

See for yourself. Visit the following web address where you can download for free our simple and easy to use Bully Premium Calculator. You need to know your company's salary costs, number of staff and a few other easy to obtain details. Plug them into our calculator and we'll offer an expertly assessed estimate of what bullying could be costing your organisation each year.

Access the calculator at:

bully-inc.com

Made in the USA
Coppell, TX
31 August 2021

61550540R00184